William Kent, Lester Anthony Beardslee

Beardslee on Wrought-Iron and Chain-Cables

Experiments on the Strength of Wrought-Iron and of Chain-Cables

William Kent, Lester Anthony Beardslee

Beardslee on Wrought-Iron and Chain-Cables
Experiments on the Strength of Wrought-Iron and of Chain-Cables

ISBN/EAN: 9783337185718

Printed in Europe, USA, Canada, Australia, Japan

Cover: Foto ©ninafisch / pixelio.de

More available books at **www.hansebooks.com**

FRONTISPIECE.

FIG. 1.

THE PHENOMENON OF "BARKING," AS MANIFESTED BY IRONS F AND Fx. (See Page 36.)

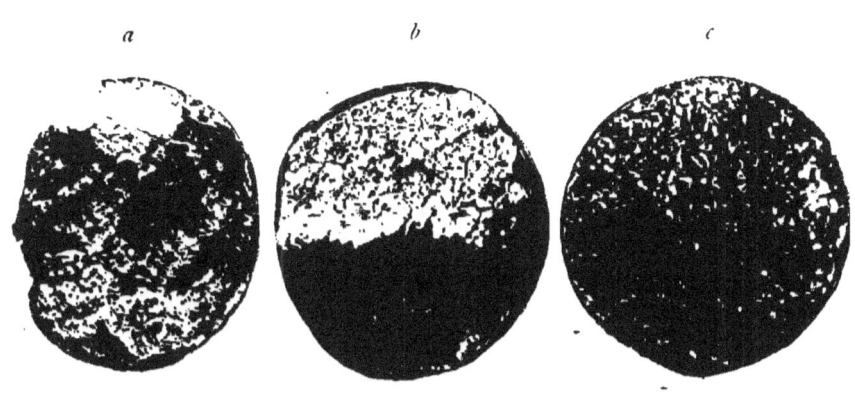

FIG. 2.

DIFFERENCE IN APPEARANCE OF FRACTURES PRODUCED BY IMPACT, OF VARYING DEGREES ENERGY, THE MATERIAL BEING THE SAME. (See Page 35.)

Heliotype Printing Co. Boston.

EXPERIMENTS

ON THE

STRENGTH OF WROUGHT-IRON

AND OF

CHAIN-CABLES.

REPORT OF THE COMMITTEES OF THE UNITED STATES BOARD APPOINTED TO TEST IRON, STEEL AND OTHER METALS, ON CHAIN-CABLES, MALLEABLE IRON, AND RE-HEATING AND RE-ROLLING WROUGHT-IRON;

INCLUDING

MISCELLANEOUS INVESTIGATIONS INTO THE PHYSICAL AND CHEMICAL PROPERTIES OF ROLLED WROUGHT-IRON.

BY

COMMANDER L. A. BEARDSLEE, U.S.N.,

Member of the Board, and Chairman of the Committees.

Revised and Abridged

BY

WILLIAM KENT, M.E.,

Formerly Assistant to the Committee on Alloys of the United States Board; Associate Editor of the "American Manufacturer and Iron World," Pittsburgh, Penn.

NEW YORK:
JOHN WILEY AND SONS,
15 ASTOR PLACE.
1879.

PREFACE.

The Report of which the following pages are an abridgment was published by the United States Government in 1879, as part of Executive Document No. 98, House of Representatives, Forty-fifth Congress, Second Session.

It forms an octavo of two hundred and sixty-seven pages, with thirteen heliotype-plates, and several wood-cuts. It is not only by far the most elaborate record of tests of wrought-iron and of chain-cables that has ever been given to the world, but it is the most valuable in results; in describing newly observed phenomena, in tabulating variations of strength due to differences in methods of manufacture, and revealing their causes, in investigation of the effect of impact, in pointing out causes of defects in strength of both bars and cables, and generally in giving information that is of immediate practical value to manufacturers of iron and to engineers.

As but a limited number of copies of the report were issued by the Government, and as it contains a large amount of detailed tabular matter, which, while necessary in an official report of this kind, to corroborate the conclusions deduced, is not necessary to a full comprehension of these conclusions, — it has been thought that an abridgment would be acceptable to many who would be unable to obtain the original work.

The undersigned, in preparing the abridgment, has had the full consent of Commander Beardslee, and obtained his approval of the manuscript prior to publication.

WM. KENT.

Pittsburgh, Penn., May, 1879.

CONTENTS.

SECTION I.

	PAGE
INTRODUCTION	1
THE BAR. — PART I.	4
Testing-Machines, and Methods of Testing	5
Notes upon the "Records of Bars tested by Tension"	6
Strength and Elastic Limit of Round Bar-Iron	8
THE BAR. — PART II.	11
Investigation of the Effect of Differences in the Amount of Reduction by the Rolls	11

SECTION II.

PART I. — PROPER FORM AND PROPORTIONS OF TEST-PIECES	20
PART II. — COMPARATIVE STRENGTH OF BARS IN THEIR NORMAL CONDITION, AND AS REDUCED BY TURNING AWAY THE SKIN AND ADJACENT IRON	27

SECTION III.

TESTS OF BARS BY IMPACT; SHOWING ACTION OF VARIOUS TYPES OF IRON UNDER SUDDEN STRAINS	31
Method of testing by Impact	32
Barking	36
Crystallization	36
Record of Impact Tests	37

SECTION IV.

A PAPER DESCRIBING A SERIES OF EXPERIMENTS TO DETERMINE FACTS IN REGARD TO THE OPERATION OF THE LAW CALLED THE ELEVATION OF THE LIMIT OF STRESS	40

SECTION V.

THE CABLE	49
Experiments upon Comparative Strength of Studded and Unstudded Links	52
Description of Method of testing Cables	54
Weight of Chain-Cables	57
Methods by which the Weight of Chain-Cables can be reduced in a greater Ratio than the Strength	58
Comparison of Results obtained by Tension upon Sections of Cable-Links, and upon Bars of the Iron from which Links were made	62

SECTION VI.

PROOF-STRAINS FOR CHAIN-CABLES	68
Effects of the Use of Strains prescribed by the Admiralty Proof-Table	68
Discussion of the Principles upon which Proof-Strains should be based	71
Ratio of Strength of Sections of Links to that of the Bars from which they were made	72
Probable Strength of Round Bars, calculated with an Allowance for Variation in Strength due to Variation in Diameter . .	77
Probable Strength of Cables made from Bars of given Strength .	79
Recommended Proof-Table	81
Comparison of the Proof-Strains recommended, and the Strains in Use	81

SECTION VII.

PART I.—NOTES UPON THE IRONS EXAMINED	83
PART II.—COMPARISON OF CHEMICAL AND PHYSICAL RESULTS . .	92
Analyses of the Irons used in making Chain-Cables . . .	93
Relative Values of Iron in Bars, in Tenacity, Reduction of Area, and Elongation, and in Proportion of Chain to Bar . . .	95
Summary of the Principal Physical and Chemical Properties of Sixteen Irons	96
Effects of Phosphorus	97
Effects of Silicon	101
Effects of Carbon	102
Effects of Manganese, Copper, Nickel, Cobalt, Sulphur, and Slag,	105
Welding	106
What is learned from Chemical Analyses	113
Conclusions derived from a Comparison of Chemical and Physical Results	117

REPORT

OF THE

RESULTS OF INVESTIGATIONS MADE BY COMMITTEES D, H, AND M, OF THE UNITED-STATES BOARD APPOINTED TO TEST IRON, STEEL, AND OTHER METALS.

SECTION I.

INTRODUCTION.

THE investigations assigned to the three committees designated by the letters D, H, and M were as follows: —

To Committee D, "On Chain and Wire Ropes," with instructions "to determine the character of iron best adapted for chain cables, the best form and proportions of link, and the qualities of metal used in the manufacture of iron and steel wire rope."

To Committee H, "On Iron, Malleable," with instructions "to examine and report upon the mechanical and physical properties of wrought-iron."

To Committee M, "On Re-heating and Re-rolling," with instructions "to examine and report upon the effects of re-heating and re-rolling, or otherwise re-working, of hammering as compared with rolling, and of annealing the metals."

The work thus assigned to three different committees was of such a nature, that experiments made by any one of them would necessarily furnish data which would prove of value to all; and as the three committees consisted of but five members of the board, one of whom was chairman of all, it was considered advisable, in order to economize time, labor, and means by the avoidance of duplication of expensive experiments, and of making duplicate and triplicate reports of the same series, to consolidate the committees, and to conduct the investigations in such a manner that a single report would cover the whole ground. In thus concentrating the work, it was necessary that a leading object should be selected, and it was considered that the research required to establish the characteristics of iron best adapted for the manufacture of cables would furnish data which would bear more or less upon the subjects to be investigated by Committees H and M; while it would be quite practicable to select from the wide field presented by "wrought-iron," and differences in methods of treating it, any number of lines of research, none of which would prove of much service in establishing points in regard to chain-iron.

Our experiments, therefore, have been all so carried out, that while we have been able to obtain data, both as to the mechanical and physical properties of wrought-iron, and as to the effects of different methods of treatment of the raw material, all have been made to contribute their quota toward the establishment of methods by which an iron could be judged correctly as to its adaptability for chain-cable manufacture. Such points well established would prove to possess value, not only to the manufacturers and purchasers of cables and cable-iron, but also to manufacturers of iron bridges and other constructions, which, like the cable, depend for their value upon their power of resisting to the utmost destroying forces of various and irregular natures.

In submitting this report, we would say that the extent of our investigations has been restricted by narrowness of our means, and the necessity which has arisen that we should submit the results of such work as we have accomplished. They but point the way toward a thorough re-examination of the subjects involved, which, based upon our results, would provide a valuable mass of information, to which this report would occupy the relation of a preface.

The cable-link is but a modification of the round rolled bar, and its qualities must depend upon those of the bar from which it is made. Therefore we have selected the ROUND BAR as the foundation of our work; and our endeavor has been to ascertain what qualities should be inherent in it, and which should remain without deterioration through various processes incident to the manufacture from it of finished products of other forms.

Cables in service are subject to the destroying forces of sudden strains, alternations of sudden and steady heavy strains, heavy steady strains, abrasion, and corrosion; and the danger from each takes precedence in the order given.

The relative importance of these sources of danger indicates that iron which is best adapted for cables is that which possesses great power to resist *both* sudden and steady strains, and that neither of these qualities in excess will compensate for a deficiency in the other.

The strength of the cable is but that of the weakest link, and the strength of this link but that of the *weakest part:* therefore, in order that a cable shall be strong and reliable, the weakest part of the weakest link must be made as strong as possible.

The weakest part of nearly every link is the *weld*. With certain types of iron the weld is much weaker than with others: hence we consider that the prime elements of value in a cable-iron are power to *resist sudden strains*, and to be *welded thoroughly* without loss of strength. By the former we insure against the greatest danger, and by the latter against the frequently repeated ordinary dangers.

We were not able to obtain any information of value as to the qualities of various American irons in these two respects; and we therefore resolved upon making a series of experimental investigations, by the results of which we hoped to be able to form a correct judgment.

THE BAR. — PART I.

Our plan of investigation was to first ascertain, by means of tension tests made upon bars of such irons as we could procure, the amount of strength, elasticity, &c., which would be found to exist in ordinary American bar iron; next, by tests by impact upon the same irons, to ascertain their relative powers to resist sudden strains; and finally, having ascertained these essential points in the *material*, to make from each iron a number of cable-links, and by tension to find their strength and uniformity, and the degree of dependence to be placed upon the *welds*.

To carry out these investigations, we procured bars of round iron of sizes such as are usually used in the manufacture of cables; viz., from two-inch diameter to one inch, from the following rolling-mills and dealers in iron, viz., Burden & Sons of New York, Bentoni of Pennsylvania, Burgess of Ohio, Catasauqua of Pennsylvania, New-Jersey Iron and Steel Company of New Jersey, Niles Iron Company of Ohio, Phœnix of Pennsylvania, Pembroke of Massachusetts, Pencoyd of Pennsylvania, Tredegar of Virginia, Trego and Thompson of Maryland, Sligo of Pennsylvania, Tamaqua of Pennsylvania, Wyeth Brothers of Maryland, and many other bars of unknown origin.

The experiments, upon the results of which our report is based, comprise the details of all physical phenomena observed by us while testing to destruction nearly two thousand bar test-pieces by the strain of tension, over fifteen hundred by the strain of percussion, and nearly five hundred cable-links, made in all respects as for service.

The tension-tests upon bars were made both upon bars in their normal condition, and upon others from which a portion of the surface had been turned away. Those by impact were made upon portions of the same bars which had been tested by tension, and those upon chain-links from other portions of the same bars. The Navy Department placed at our service the facilities of the Washington Navy Yard, which included the use of forges and of two testing-machines for making tension-tests; also of such records as we desired, and of a large quantity of contract chain-iron, which it was deemed advisable to examine.

A brief description of our testing-machines, and of our methods of testing, with a few physical phenomena we have observed, will enable the terms used in the report to be understood.

Testing-Machines, and Methods of Testing.

In order that we might obtain the tensile strength, elastic limit, ductility, &c., of round bars, our first test was by tension upon full-sized bars, from which the outer portion had not been removed. These tests were made by means of the "chain-proving machine," at the Washington Navy Yard, which in this report is called "testing-machine A." This machine consists of a long trough, in which a fifteen-fathom section of cable can be stretched by means of a hydraulic pump, to which it is connected at one end, while the other end is made fast to a holder, which in turn connects with a system of levers, by which the stress is weighed by means of weights placed upon a platform at the extremity of the long lever.

The capacity of the machine is three hundred thousand pounds, and the levers are so adjusted that a weight of one pound upon the platform balances two hundred pounds of stress.

The pieces to be tested were sections of the bar at least eight times the diameter in length, and originally fitted with loops of larger-sized iron, welded to the ends.

Additional tests by tension were made upon many of the irons by means of cylindrical test-pieces turned from the bars, and ruptured by the "Rodman Dynamometer," called in this report "testing-machine B."

The results obtained by this machine agree very closely, in some cases, with those obtained by testing-machine A, and in others differ widely. A portion of these differences is probably due to differences in the accuracy of the two machines and methods, and others to a natural difference in the character of the metal as developed by the entire bar, and by a portion of the core and adjacent iron.

This machine holds the specimen to be tested by means of clamps.

The capacity of the machine is one hundred thousand pounds, and it will weigh a stress of ten pounds with accuracy.

NOTES UPON THE "RECORDS OF BARS TESTED BY TENSION."

Column headed "Diameter." — The strength per square inch of a bar, as deduced from the stress at which the entire bar has been torn asunder, cannot be correctly ascertained, except the diameter of the bar be carefully calipered: the *nominal* size and the exact size seldom coincide; and at times we have found variations of four-hundredths of an inch, which variation is sufficient to produce important errors.

Areas. — The "original area" is that which corresponds to the diameter of the piece before test; the "reduced area" corresponds with the least diameter after rupture; the "tensile limit area" corresponds with the least diameter at the highest stress the piece sustains.

Length. — The length of the clear cylindrical portion between punch-marks is measured before the stress is applied, and after fracture. In testing with the machine B it is also measured at the "tensile limit."

Percentage of Elongation. — This element, as given in many tables, is of little value, the percentage being greatly dependent upon the original length of the specimen. When this is not given, the percentage is of no value.

The following experiment will make this clear: From a bar of $1\frac{3}{4}''$ iron, of very uniform character, three test-pieces were prepared, which were in all respects similar, except in length. The first was 75, the second 20, and the third 10 inches long.

They were pulled asunder, and the first was found to have elongated 14 inches, or 18.64 per cent of the original length; the second had elongated 4.36 inches, or 21.8 per cent; and the third 2.22 inches, or 22.2 per cent. Our records supply many confirmatory results.

First Stretch. — The bar being fastened to the holders, a pair of large dividers was adjusted to punch-marks, and the stress slowly applied; at the instant the elongation was sufficient to draw one punch-mark clear of the dividers' point, the stress was weighed, and recorded as *first stretch.*

Ultimate stress is the stress which represents the highest which has been withstood by the specimen; but it was not the amount which finally produced the rupture: this stress produced a weakening, from which, had the specimen been rested, it would have recovered; by continuing it, the specimen finally parted at much less.

Original, Fractured, and Tensile Limit Areas. — The measurements taken at the "tensile limit" introduce a new method by which the comparative values of different irons may be estimated.

Ordinarily the tenacity of iron is expressed in the strength per square inch of the sectional area of the test-piece before its form has been changed by stress.

Kirkaldy suggested, as a more just method, that the area corresponding to the diameter of the fractured surfaces should be adopted as the limit of measurement.

Our experiments lead us to believe that between these extremes of original and fractured areas there is an intermediate area which can be used with profit, *which is that which corresponds with the least diameter of the test-piece at the stress which marks the highest point of resistance to continually increasing strains.* This point we have termed the "*tensile limit.*"

There are practical difficulties encountered in measuring accurately the diameter of the fractured surfaces. After the test-piece has been pulled asunder, there is a difficulty in joining perfectly the two fractured surfaces, and frequently the line of surface is not at right angles with the axis of the cylinder: this necessitates two measurements, — one of the greatest and one of the least diameter, and an interpolation, — and, in making these measurements, there are chances of error, even if the line of fracture is at right angles, which are increased when it is not.

The tensile strength per square inch of original area is more liable to be free from errors arising from inaccuracy than is that of the fractured area. But neither of these measurements provides us with a standard by which we can judge of the relative amount of change of form that takes place with different irons at the moment when they *finally cease to resist* an increase of stress; this deficiency is supplied in the area at the tensile limit, which area corresponds to the diameter of the test-piece, at the instant when affected by the highest stress the material is capable of resisting, and not by subsequent stress applied to a rapidly-yielding metal.

Length of Test-Piece. — Not only the "percentage of elongation" obtained by testing a piece of iron, but the strength, depends upon the length of the test-piece. Our experiments show, that, if an iron is judged by a test-piece whose length is less than four diameters, the judgment is wrong.

STRENGTH AND ELASTIC LIMIT OF ROUND BAR-IRON.

In the following table the stresses by tension required to rupture many of the bars we have tested are arranged in their relative order, the greatest stress required being given precedence upon each size.

In the columns in which the stress is reduced to the square inch, the areas corresponding to the actual diameters of the bars have been used. This gives a more correct estimate of the relative order of tenacity than the diameter given in the first column, by using which bars would frequently gain or lose

THE BAR.

in precedence on account of excess or lack of material, some being rolled "full," and others "scant."

In the column "Standard for Size," the strength which we have found best adapted for cable-iron is placed for comparison.

The elastic limit as given is not from perfectly accurate data: it is simply the amount of stress which produced the first perceptible change of form, divided by the bar's area.

Strength per Original Area, per Square Inch, and Elastic Limit per Square Inch, of 959 Round Bars.

Diameter.	Name of Iron.	Number of Tests.	Strength.		Elastic Limit per Square Inch.	Standard for Size.	Diameter.	Name of Iron.	Number of Tests.	Strength.		Elastic Limit per Square Inch.	Standard for Size.
			Original Area.	Per Square Inch.						Original Area.	Per Square Inch.		
in.			lbs.	lbs.	lbs.	lbs.	in.			lbs.	lbs.	lbs.	lbs.
¼	F	1	2,920	59,585	....		1⅛	N	2	56,200	56,143	32,267	
⅜	F.	4	5,886	54,090	40,980			Fx2	3	55,100	55,927	37,250	
½	C	6	12,311	62,700	....			E	1	55,142	53,097	33,549	
	C	7	11,609	50,000	....			Fx3	2	54,900	54,644	34,695	
	C	8	11,388	57,700	....			D	2	54,360	54,687	28,166	
	C	11	10,861	55,400	....			A	3	53,907	53,900	26,787	
	F	1	10,359	52,275	39,126			F	3	53,050	53,850	33,457	
⅝	F	11	16,977	55,450	....			O	1	50,400	53,035	32,410	
	F	4	15,928	52,050	....			F	2	50,300	50,149	35,493	
	F	11	17,644	57,660	....			F	5	49,660	52,267	32,019	
¾	F	4	22,746	51,546	35,933		1¼	K	2	72,960	59,461	36,501	65,914
⅞	F	4	30,850	50,630	33,931			P	2	73,200	56,876	36,868	
								C	1	71,040	57,897	32,469	
								D	2	72,300	57,977	31,996	
								P	2	70,704	55,782	35,596	
								Px	2	70,250	56,334	33,921	
1	K	13	48,480	61,727	....	43,665		N	2	69,300	56,478	33,251	
	D	1	48,000	61,115	33,486			Fx1	5	68,460	55,253	34,784	
	O	1	46,000	57,363	37,415			D	1	68,160	55,550	28,166	
	Fx1	5	45,040	55,768	34,729			E	1	67,200	53,893	32,712	
	P	2	44,500	57,807	39,230			Fx2	3	66,000	55,132	38,603	
	A	3	44,126	54,690	34,881			Fx3	2	66,400	53,247	32,520	
	Fx2	3	44,450	56,790	36,585			A	3	66,112	53,897	27,643	
	Fx3	2	42,350	53,915	36,336			M	20	65,960	53,752	....	
	F	2	41,600	51,921	31,300			M	20	65,850	54,000	....	
	D	8	41,547	52,900	....			F	2	64,990	52,070	32,075	
	F	5	40,660	52,819	32,267			F	2	64,700	52,729	39,608	
	F	4	40,309	51,400	34,600			M	20	64,285	53,022	....	
								F	5	62,520	52,620	33,220	
								O	1	61,400	50,040	30,730	
1⅛	K	3	60,096	60,458	37,344	54,261							
	D	1	58,700	59,582	33,597		1 5/16	P	94	74,427	54,518	35,898	72,183
	C	2	57,125	57,470	31,900								
	Fx1	5	57,620	56,434	34,682		1⅜	M	48	86,862	58,926	37,548	78,607
	P	2	56,500	57,496	41,311			M	35	87,496	57,649	38,578	

WROUGHT-IRON AND CHAIN-CABLES.

Diameter.	Name of Iron.	Number of Tests.	Strength.		Elastic Limit per Square Inch.	Standard for Size.	Diameter.	Name of Iron.	Number of Tests.	Strength.		Elastic Limit per Square Inch.	Standard for Size.
			Original Area.	Per Square Inch.						Original Area.	Per Square Inch.		
in.			*lbs.*	*lbs.*	*lbs.*	*lbs.*	*in.*			*lbs.*	*lbs.*	*lbs.*	*lbs.*
1⅜	D	1	86,800	58,021	32,152		1⅝	Px	2	115,500	54,689	33,427	
	K	2	82,248	55,790	31,034			A	2	111,984	54,334	32,163	
	C	1	81,600	54,949	31,030			D	1	111,360	53,695	30,087	
	M	28	80,693	54,373	35,820			Fx3	2	111,300	53,339	33,540	
	N	2	81,200	54,277	33,622			Fx1	5	110,140	53,537	34,335	
	Fx1	5	80,360	52,968	33,275			D	1	110,500	53,614	30,664	
	Fx3	2	80,000	52,733	34,606			J	1	109,400	52,748	....	
	E	1	79,296	52,254	25,930			E	1	109,245	52,675	33,745	
	A	3	78,994	53,557	33,650			Fx2	3	108,800	53,483	35,870	
	P	1	78,624	52,556	30,802			H	1	108,500	52,314	29,364	
	F	5	78,580	52,537	34,469			E	1	108,384	51,946	27,695	
	F	2	78,300	52,339	39,103			O	1	108,000	52,401	34,012	
	M	4	78,150	53,016	35,379			F	2	107,520	52,163	33,907	
	Fx2	3	76,333	51,487	35,911			G	1	106,200	51,205	33,318	
	F	2	77,235	51,296	31,992			F	2	105,500	50,529	35,390	
	O	1	72,400	50,594	34,940			F	2	105,440	50,970	33,625	
								C	1	101,700	49,030	31,099	
1 7⁄16	P	1	89,300	53,345	....	85,339							
	E	1	87,552	53,944	32,542		1 11⁄16	K	1	130,000	56,595	38,310	114,770
	G	1	86,400	53,238	32,534			B-	1	121,150	54,181	....	
	B	4	84,862	52,287	32,411			J	1	121,000	54,114	....	
	C	1	84,000	51,756	32,655			B	3	118,273	52,895	33,145	
	J	1	81,800	50,400	....			E	1	116,544	52,120	35,549	
								G	1	115,800	57,789	34,160	
1½	M	12	102,125	57,052	38,417	92,322		C	1	111,400	49,821	83,184	
	K	2	101,280	57,317	33,412								
	D	1	101,200	56,505	32,496		1¾	K	1	139,200	57,874	....	122,745
	M	25	99,064	55,466	34,780			Px	2	131,900	54,212	33,908	
	M	26	98,730	55,131	33,771			C	5	130,836	54,410	31,354	
	P	2	98,300	54,159	33,140			P	2	130,050	52,844	33,642	
	M	17	98,047	54,540	....			Fx1	5	129,500	53,846	36,573	
	C	4	97,921	55,404	34,770			H	1	129,400	53,800	27,856	
	E	1	97,920	55,415	32,869			N	2	129,350	55,018	34,283	
	M	20	97,665	54,816	34,716			D	1	128,600	53,472	31,892	
	Px	2	97,350	54,354	34,617			J	1	128,100	53,264	....	
	M	27	97,095	54,095	35,544			D	1	126,720	52,699	27,817	
	E	1	96,384	54,544	33,027			Fx3	2	126,100	53,154	35,323	
	P	1	95,904	52,868	29,636			E	2	124,128	51,606	26,541	
	M	20	95,810	53,512	....			A	2	123,340	51,509	29,404	
	M	23	94,809	52,941	....			F	1	121,920	50,690	32,229	
	Fx3	2	94,600	52,819	34,840			G	1	121,200	50,395	36,254	
	Fx1	5	94,520	53,491	34,807			C	2	121,000	50,312	30,852	
	M	4	93,500	52,736	34,901			C	2	120,200	50,547	35,954	
	N	2	93,400	53,555	34,690			Fx2	3	120,167	52,314	35,320	
	C	1	93,100	52,700	35,880			E	1	119,808	49,616	31,214	
	H	1	92,700	52,462	29,992			F	5	117,740	49,738	28,907	
	D	1	92,160	52,155	27,708			O	1	116,500	50,129	32,271	
	A	2	91,680	51,854	28,794								
	F	2	91,875	51,994	32,054		1 13⁄16	K	1	148,800	56,577	....	130,965
	O	1	91,400	50,919	32,312			B	4	138,507	53,655	....	
	F	5	90,925	51,456	34,591			J	1	131,500	50,969	30,814	
	Fx2	3	90,967	51,481	34,917			G	1	129,850	50,310	33,565	
	J	1	90,200	51,047	....			E	1	129,792	50,307	29,767	
	M	1	87,100	49,292	32,597			J	1	126,300	48,953	....	
1⅝	N	2	119,000	56,344	35,889	107,040	1⅞	K	2	154,080	55,803	31,031	139,430
	K	4	118,463	57,132	35,026			C	5	150,336	54,447	32,334	
	M	10	119,800	57,402	35,701			D	1	149,000	53,100	32,074	
	M	2	117,500	55,634	33,522			N	1	148,350	54,004	33,610	
	P	4	116,892	56,227	33,207			Fx1	5	146,780	52,875	35,641	

THE BAR.

Diameter.	Name of Iron.	Number of Tests.	Strength. Original Area.	Strength. Per Square Inch.	Elastic Limit per Square Inch.	Standard for Size.	Diameter.	Name of Iron.	Number of Tests.	Strength. Original Area.	Strength. Per Square Inch.	Elastic Limit per Square Inch.	Standard for Size.
in.			lbs.	lbs.	lbs.	lbs.	in.			lbs.	lbs.	lbs.	lbs.
1⅞	Fx3	2	146,500	53,361	35,032		2	F	5	149,960	47,569	28,792	
	P	2	145,200	52,505	32,312			O	2	151,540	48,249	31,413	
	E	2	142,900	50,880	27,100			D	1	149,800	49,146	33,068	
	D	1	142,080	51,459	27,816			D	1	142,100	46,151	36,050	
	Px	2	142,000	51,762	32,261								
	M	2	141,300	50,363	....		2 1/16	M	1	178,600	51,559	....	
	A	2	141,120	50,584	28,713			M	1	171,200	49,422	....	
	F	2	140,925	51,039	33,067								
	Fx2	3	139,000	51,150	33,970		2⅛	M	1	184,800	50,481	....	
	F	2	136,600	49,744	35,615			M	1	186,000	51,225	....	
	F	3	134,500	49,355	32,855			A	1	170,784	48,382	30,459	
	F	2	132,250	48,670	23,250								
	O	1	129,000	47,478	30,842		2 3/16	M	2	200,000	51,666	....	
1 15/16	M	1	156,000	51,707	....	148,137	2¼	M	1	210,400	51,530	....	
	M	2	155,300	51,474	....			M	1	205,800	51,296	....	
	M	1	154,000	51,242	....			F	3	195,977	49,290	32,163	
								F	2	195,478	49,164	31,966	
2	K	1	194,880	60,213	31,441	157,080		F	2	192,700	48,898	....	
	K	1	188,160	57,567	30,839			F	1	189,600	48,812	....	
	P'x	2	167,900	52,914	31,198			P	2	184,700	46,866	28,241	
	M	1	167,600	52,820	....								
	M	1	156,000	49,164	....		2½	F	2	237,930	48,475	28,932	
	E	1	167,712	51,818	27,318			F	3	232,776	47,428	29,941	
	P	2	165,600	51,684	33,104			F	2	232,400	47,344	29,758	
	P	2	161,300	50,834	31,878								
	N	1	165,400	52,127	32,461		2¾	F	3	275,889	46,446	26,333	
	N	1	163,000	51,370	32,460								
	Fx1	5	163,420	52,011	34,702		3	F	3	337,603	47,761	26,400	
	C*	1	160,704	51,153	29,335								
	D*	1	160,700	51,146	28,567		3¼	F	2	390,019	47,014	24,591	
	P	1	159,840	49,872	29,953								
	Fx2	2	155,500	50,000	36,184		3½	F	2	452,191	47,000	24,961	
	Fx3	2	159,500	50,763	33,172								
	A	9	157,588	50,171	28,083		3¾	F	2	515,423	46,667	23,636	
	F	2	152,260	48,596	27,634								
	F	2	151,900	47,812	35,864		4	F	2	582,100	46,322	23,430	

THE BAR.—PART II.

INVESTIGATION OF THE EFFECT OF DIFFERENCES IN THE AMOUNT OF REDUCTION BY THE ROLLS.

In procuring material upon which to make tests by tension both in the bar and link form, our custom was to purchase from manufacturers at least one bar of each size ordinarily used in chain-cables. Testing these bars in their normal condition by tension, it became evident that the strength of the different sizes was not in proportion to their areas; but that, on the contrary, there existed a variation in proportional strength which was in accord with variations in the diameter of the bars. In general terms it was found, that, as the diameter of the bar became less, the strength per square inch increased; but, in comparing the results obtained from a number of such sets of bars, it became evident that the increase of strength from between the two extremes of, say, 2″ and 1″ was not created by a series of uniform steps upon each successive reduction, but that there was one point in the reduction where a *decrease* took the place of the usual increase, and that from this point the increase again began, and generally by more rapid steps.

Thus the 2″ bar was of less strength than the $1\frac{7}{8}$″; the latter was of less than the $1\frac{3}{4}$″, which was, in turn, less than the $1\frac{5}{8}$″, but the strength of the $1\frac{5}{8}$″ was greater than that of the $1\frac{1}{2}$″; the $1\frac{3}{8}$″, $1\frac{1}{4}$″, $1\frac{1}{8}$″, and sometimes the 1″, being each of increased strength in the order given.

We found, that, with a set of bars of the above sizes, the difference in proportional strength between the extremes was from four to six thousand pounds; that the tenacity of the $1\frac{5}{8}$″ exceeded that of the 2″ from two to three thousand pounds, and that of the $1\frac{1}{2}$″ from one to three thousand pounds.

As we became fully satisfied that these variations *did* exist in all uniform irons which we examined, we considered ourselves justified in assuming that they would probably occur generally with other irons, and that, so occurring, their existence should be taken into consideration in any attempt to calculate the strength of links or other articles made from bar-iron of various sizes.

Experiments at the testing-machine afforded no indications by which we could determine any thing in regard to the causes of these variations. We therefore undertook to watch all the processes connected with the manufacture of a "set of bars," in hopes that while so doing we should be able to detect the hidden reason.

At our first visit to a rolling-mill, a set of bars were prepared of carefully selected material, and careful notes were taken during the process of manufacture, which are herewith reproduced. There were two bars of each size rolled.

Notes in Regard to Manufacture of Iron F, Second Lot.

Size of Bar.	Dimensions of Piles.	Time in Furnace.	Number of Passes.		Time in Rolls.	Size of Bar.	Dimensions of Piles.	Time in Furnace.	Number of Passes.		Time in Rolls.
			Square Rolls.	Round Rolls.					Square Rolls.	Round Rolls.	
		h.m.			m.			h.m.			m.
2″	6″ x 10″ x 26″	2.06	15	9	09	1½	6″ x 6″ x 26″	1.32	13	8	05½
2	6 x 10 x 26	2.15	15	9	08	1⅜	6 x 6 x 21	1.00	15	8	05
1⅞	6 x 10 x 24	2.02	15	9	07	1⅜	6 x 6 x 21	1.04	15	8	04
1⅞	6 x 10 x 24	2.23	15	8	07	1¼	6 x 6 x 14	1.20	15	8	04
1¾	6 x 10 x 21	1.40	17	9	07	1¼	6 x 6 x 14	1.20	15	8	04
1¾	6 x 10 x 21	1.49	17	9	06	1⅛	6 x 6 x 12	1.10	15	8	04
1⅝	6 x 10 x 18	1.35	15	9	06	1⅛	6 x 6 x 12	1.10	15	8	04
1⅝	6 x 10 x 18	1.40	15	9	06	1	6 x 4 x 14	1.10	15	8	04
1½	6 x 6 x 26	1.26	13	10	05	1	6 x 4 x 14	1.10	15	8	04

A study of these notes indicated that if there proved to exist any marked difference in the characteristics of the different bars, it could not be considered as owing to want of care in their preparation. No accident caused delays while passing through the rolls, and the number of passes was quite uniform.

By contrasting the areas of these piles with those of the resulting bars, it will be seen that there was a very different amount of reduction produced by the rolls, varying from 5.23 to 2.76 per cent. The tenacity of these bars agreed to some extent with the amount of reduction, but not so closely as had been expected.

The experiment was repeated by watching another set of bars rolled by the same mill, of the same material, the set comprising bars of all sizes, ranging by ⅛″ from 4″ diameter to ¼″ diameter. The iron was very carefully heated, and received a nearly uniform number of passes through the rolls.

The dimensions of the piles, the proportion borne by the areas of the resultant bars, and the tensile strength and elastic limit per square inch of the bars, as found by tests made upon them entire and upon cylinders turned from the cores, are given in the following table.

Iron F, Third Lot.

Comparisons of the Reductions by the Rolls, with the Effects upon Tenacity and Elastic Limit, of Iron F, Third Lot.

Size of Bar.	Area of Pile.	Area of Bar in per cent of area of Pile.	Tensile Strength.		Elastic Limit.	
			Entire Bar.	Core.	Entire Bar.	Core.
	Sq. In.	Per cent.	Pounds.	Pounds.	Pounds.	Pounds.
4	80	15.70	.....	46,322	.....	23,430
3¾	80	13.80	.....	46,667	.....	23,636
3½	80	12.03	.....	47,000	.....	24,961
3¼	80	10.37	.....	47,014	.....	24,591
3	80	8.83	.....	47,761	.....	26,400
2¾	80	7.42	.....	46,466	.....	26,333
2½	80	6.13	47,344	47,428	29,758	29,941
2¼	72	5.52	48,505	49,290	31,267	32,163
2	72	4.36	47,872	48,280	35,864	31,892
1⅞	36	7.67	49,744	49,370	35,615	37,042
1¾	36	6.08	50,547	48,792	35,954	38,992
1⅝	36	5.76	50,529	49,144	35,394	34,208
1½	36	4.90	50,820	51,838	35,087	36,467
1⅜	36	4.12	52,339	48,819	30,103	.....
1¼	36	3.41	52,729	49,801	39,608	40,534
1⅛	25	3.96	50,149	50,530	35,493	37,771
1	25	3.14	51,921	51,128	39,066	38,596
⅞	12¼	4.91	50,716	50,374	33,931	33,931
¾	12¼	3.60	50,673	50,276	33,933	35,933
⅝	12¼	2.50	52,297	51,431	34,450	34,545
½	9	2.17	52,275	52,775	38,445	39,126
⅜	9	3.68	54,098	54,108	38,475	40,098
¼	3	1.60	57,000	59,585	Lost	Lost

A study of the table shows first that upon the nine successively decreasing sizes, viz., from 4″ to 2″, there was but one exception to a constant rise in *tenacity* accompanying the increase of reduction by the rolls, and that the elastic limit rose upon each successive step with two exceptions, which are very slight, it falling off 350 pounds in one and 67 pounds in another instance; the tenacity of the 2″ (4.36 per cent of pile) being over that of the 4″ (15.70 per cent of pile) 1,106 pounds, and the elastic limit 8,462 pounds.

From the 1⅞″ (7.67 per cent of pile) to the 1¼″ (3.41 per cent of pile), the iron was somewhat irregular, and there was but a slight rise in tenacity, viz., 431 pounds, but in the elastic limit the rise was 4,993 pounds.

The tenacity of the ⅞" (4.91 per cent of pile) was but 104 pounds greater than that of the 1⅛" (4.90 per cent of pile), that of the ⅝" (2.50 per cent of pile) nearly corresponding with that of the 1⅜" (4.12 per cent of pile).

The effect of reduction was most marked on the smaller sizes, the ½" (2.17 per cent of pile) having nearly 5,000 pounds less tenacity than the ¼" (1.60 per cent of pile).

The notes taken at the mill do not indicate that either bar was under or over heated; but there are indications that the 1½" bar was *overheated*, inasmuch as the strength of the core exceeded that of the entire bar.

So far as this experiment was expected to account for the usually found greater strength of the 1⅝" bar, it proved a failure, for it was weaker than the bars immediately succeeding or preceding; but we considered that the information gained as to the probable effect of *under* and *over* heating was of value. The indications are that if a bar is *underheated* it will have an unduly high tenacity and elastic limit, and that if *overheated* the reverse will be the case; further, if *underheated* the strength obtained by a cylinder turned from the core will be less than that which would be obtained by testing the entire bar, if the diameter be small, and greater if the cylinder is turned from a large bar.

It is possible that the above two points are interdependent, as the large bars are more apt to be irregularly heated than the small ones, and some portions of the pile must be in a state fit to roll before other portions are sufficiently heated; these *overheated* portions we turn off from the bar to produce the cylindrical test-piece.

As in the previous experiment, we believed that the thorough work received by all sizes put them in condition which prevented the effect due to a slight difference in the reduction being plainly manifest. We therefore selected for another experiment the bars of a very slightly worked iron; viz., iron N.

Iron N.

Dimensions of Piles, Areas of Piles, of Bars in percentage of Areas of Piles, Tenacity, Elastic Limit, &c., of Iron N.

Size of Bars.	Dimensions of Piles.	Area of Piles.	Area of Bars in per cent of Area of Piles.	Tensile Strength.	Elastic Limit.
		Sq. In.	Per cent.	Pounds.	Pounds.
2″	6″ × 4¾″ × 26″	27	11.63	51,848	32,461
1⅞	6 × 4¾ × 21	27	10.22	54,034	33,610
1¾	6 × 4¾ × 21	27	8.90	55,018	34,283
1⅝	6 × 4¾ × 16½	27	7.68	56,344	35,889
1½	4 × 3¾ × 25	15	11.78	53,550	34,690
1⅜	4 × 3¾ × 23	15	9.90	54,277	33,622
1¼	4 × 3¾ × 17	15	8.18	56,478	33,251
1⅛	4 × 3¾ × 16	15	6.62	56,143	32,267

The above results supplied the missing evidence. With one exception, the tenacity and elastic limit increased upon each successive increase in the amount of reduction by the rolls, as shown more plainly thus, where they are arranged in the order of their reduction: 1⅛″ (6.62 per cent of pile), 56,543; 1⅝″ (7.68 per cent of pile), 56,344; 1¼″ (8.18 per cent of pile), 56,478; 1¾″ (8.90 per cent of pile), 55,018; 1⅜″ (9.90 per cent of pile), 54,277; 1⅞″ (10.22 per cent of pile), 54,034; 2″ (11.63 per cent of pile), 51,848; 1½″ (11.78 per cent of pile), 53,550.

The tensile strength of the 2″ bar was probably greater than recorded, the iron being so brittle that the head of the test-piece pulled off, and the bar could be broken by sledge-blows, without previous nicking. This iron, under every form of test, showed, by its marked contrast with iron F, the disadvantages which follow too little work.

The evidence submitted is of sufficient value to justify us in asserting that variations in the amount of reduction by the rolls of different bars from the same material produce fully as much difference in their physical characteristics as is produced by differences in their chemical constitution.

In order to ascertain beyond question if the rule would work in both directions, and if, by giving to a series of bars a *uniform* reduction, their tenacity, &c., would prove uniform, the following experiment was made: —

One of the leading manufacturers of the country, having placed both the facilities of his mill and as much material as we wished at our service, three sets of bars were rolled, which are termed Fx Nos. 1, 2, and 3, all of which were of the same material as iron F.

In preparing the piles for the first set, they were so graduated that the percentage of the pile's area borne by the bar should increase slightly upon each reduction in diameter of the bar; it being believed that the additional work thus given to the smaller sizes would, in a measure, counteract the possible differences which might be due to overheating of the large and underheating of the small bars.

The dimensions of piles, &c., are given in the following table, together with the tensile strength, elastic limit, &c., of the resultant bars.

Fx No. 1.

Dimensions of Piles, of Bars in per cent of Piles, Tenacity and Elastic Limit of Series of Bars, of Fx No. 1.

Size of Bars.	Dimensions of Piles.	Area of Piles.	Area of Bars in per cent of Area of Piles.	Tensile Strength.	Elastic Limit.	
In.	Inches.	Sq.In.	Per cent.	Pounds.	Pounds.	
2	8 × 10	80	3.93	52,011	34,702	
1⅞	8 × 9	72	3.83	52,874	35,641	
1¾	8 × 8	64	3.75	53,846	36,573	
1⅝	6 × 10	60	3.45	53,537	34,235	
1½	6 × 9	54	3.27	53,491	34,307	
1⅜	6 × 8	48	3.09	52,968	33,275	Average 53,121 T. S. and 34,700 E. L.
1¼	6 × 8	48	2.55	55,307	34,784	
1⅛	6 × 6	36	2.76	56,434	34,682	
1	6 × 5	30	2.62	55,770	34,279	Average 55,837 T. S. and 34,582 E. L.

The results show a nearly uniform tenacity for the first six sizes, then an increase, which remains quite uniform for the other three, the elastic limit remaining very uniform throughout.

The tenacity of the 2″ bar, rolled by the usual process (iron F, 2″), its area being 5.23 per cent of pile, was 47,569 pounds, showing an increase upon this size, by the experimental process, of 4,442 pounds; and the increase of the elastic limit, 5,910 pounds, was still more marked.

No explanation, except that they were possibly not enough heated, accounts for the increased tenacity of the 1⅛″ and the 1″ bars; and the 1¼″ was, by mistake, rolled from too large a pile.

A second attempt to produce a set of bars of uniform tenacity resulted in a complete failure, due, we were assured, to a misunderstanding in regard to heating the piles; but on a third attempt we were successful, as shown by the following table, in which the usual data are given:—

Dimensions and Areas of Piles, Areas of Bars in percentages of Piles, Tensile Strength, Elastic Limit, &c., of Nine Bars of Iron Fx No. 3.

Size of Bars.	Dimensions of Piles.	Area of Piles.	Area of Bars in per cent of Area of Piles.	Tensile Strength.	Elastic Limit.
Inches.	Inches.	Sq. In.	Per cent.	Pounds.	Pounds.
2	8 × 10	80	3.92	50,763	33,258
1⅞	8 × 10	80	3.45	53,361	35,032
1¾	8 × 9	72	3.34	53,154	35,323
1⅝	8 × 8	64	3.24	53,329	33,520
1½	6 × 9	54	3.27	52,819	34,840
1⅜	6 × 7	42	3.53	52,733	34,606
1¼	6 × 6	36	3.41	53,248	33,520
1⅛	6 × 5	30	3.31	54,648	34,695
1	5 × 5	25	3.14	53,915	36,287

The pile for the 2″ was necessarily two small, as there were no rolls in the mills which would take a larger pile. The record is, however, of value as a contrast to that of the other eight bars, the average of whose tensile strength, 53,401 pounds, and of the elastic limit, 34,365 pounds, is but slightly varied from by any of the bars.

Two practical results of value may be deduced from this investigation of the action of the rolls.

The first is, that, as important differences exist in the proportionate strength of different-sized bars made of the same material, which are due entirely to differences in the processes by which they are manufactured, and as the elimination or reduction of such differences would necessitate such a great and expensive change in the system by which the bars are produced that it is not probable that it will be often attempted, it is necessary that these differences should be taken into consideration when estimates of the strength of any structure in which rolled wrought-iron, of different sizes, is introduced, are made, and in all tables of strength based upon the strength of such bars.

Second, that, where the increased value of the bars will justify the increased expense of their production, those of 2″ diameter can be increased in tensile strength over 15,000 pounds; and it is not improbable that bars of 4″ diameter can have the strength increased over 60,000 pounds, with no loss in their power to resist sudden strains.

SECTION II.

PART I. — *A Paper showing, by many Experiments, the Correct Form and Proportion of Test-Pieces to be used in order to procure correctly the Tenacity, Elastic Limit, &c., of Various Metals.* PART II. — *A Comparison of the Strength of Bars in their Normal Condition, with the same after the Bars have been reduced by turning away the Surface.*

PART I.—FORM AND PROPORTIONS OF TEST-PIECES.

In obtaining the results introduced in the tables of records of bars tested by tension, we have used the two testing-machines A and B.

By the first, we have tested all the bars of diameter greater than one inch; and, by the latter, bars in their normal condition of less than one inch diameter, and cylinders turned from the larger bars.

Our tests made upon these cylinders gave results of tensile strength and elastic limit which were so much lower than the manufacturers of the various irons considered their products equal to, that some dissatisfaction and doubt as to their correctness were expressed.

Upon examination, we found that in nearly all cases where our results were supposed to be erroneous,—on account of a lack of coincidence with results obtained in some cases by the experiments of private testers of iron, and in others by tests made in government navy-yards, by persons presumed to be competent,—the tests whose results cast doubt upon ours had been made upon test-pieces turned from the bars to a reduced diameter, which at one point was reduced by a groove to a much less one, as shown in Fig. 1, p. 25.

FORM AND PROPORTIONS OF TEST-PIECES. 21

The errors which arise through the use of this erroneously shaped and proportioned test-piece have been frequently pointed out, first by Kirkaldy, and subsequently by C. B. Richards, member American Society of Civil Engineers; but it does not appear that even yet the errors which thus arise are fully recognized. As a case in point, the following comparisons of the strength of various-sized bars of iron F, as found by our tests, and as furnished to the manufacturers by so-called testers, will fully illustrate.

This iron is *always* of so uniform a strength and quality, that the test of one bar furnishes most valuable evidence as to the probable strength of another.

Strength per Square Inch of Iron F, as found by and as furnished to the Committee.

Size. Inches.	No. of Tests.	Strength Found.			No. of Tests.	Strength Furnished.			Difference in Averages.
		From—	To—	Average		From—	To—	Average	
		Pounds.	Pounds.	Pounds.		Pounds.	Pounds.	Pounds.	
2¾	3	46,164	46,702	46,446	5	58,434	65,357	62,540	16,094
2½	3	47,558	47,871	47,764	4	54,759	60,757	57,236	9,472
2⅜	..	.....	.....	.....	8	50,773	64,099	59,048	....
2¼	3	49,155	49,465	49,623	18	58,111	71,025	63,586	13,963
2⅛	..	.....	.....	.....	15	57,473	64,823	63,300	....
2	9	46,862	49,700	48,132	15	59,440	67,471	63,350	15,218
1⅞	8	48,370	51,300	49,048	12	57,999	66,007	63,230	....
1¾	8	48,792	50,342	50,325	..	.....	.....	.....	....
1⅝	8	49,144	51,300	51,221	12	63,116	75,545	65,083	....
1½	8	49,342	51,840	51,423	..	.....	.....	.....	....
1⅜	8	48,819	50,000	52,396	..	66,312	68,255	67,062	....

With the tabulated statement furnished, the average tensile strength of all sizes combined was given at 63,207 pounds; and the results from the sizes 1¾″ and 1⅝″ had been consolidated, also those from 1½″ and 1⅜″.

With experimenters developing by accident such a uniformity in the average tensile strength of the various sizes, it is not to be wondered at that no attention had been drawn to the variation in strength accompanying variations in diameter, which is plainly indicated in our more correctly-made experiments.

The broken test-pieces by which the results were procured were shown to us, and they were of the groove-form.

We determined to thoroughly investigate the effect upon the results which were due to variations in the proportions of the test-pieces. The stock of contract-chain on hand, all of which had been considered to be of a tensile strength of at least 60,000 pounds per square inch (the standard at that time, as it is, or was, also, of the British navy), furnished material for experiment; and a number of comparative tests were made by means of grooved test-pieces and short cylinders, with results as follows: —

Comparison of Results obtained from Chain-Iron on hand, by means of Grooved Test-Pieces and Short Turned Cylinders.

Size.	Dimensions of Test-Piece.		No. of Tests.		Tensile Strength per Square Inch.		Grooves exceed Cylinders by—		Appearance of Fracture.
	Area.	Length between Heads.	Cylinders.	Grooves.	Cylinders.	Grooves.	Pounds.	Per Cent.	
In.	Square Inch.	In.			Pounds.	Pounds.			
1	One-quarter.	1.20	3	3	57,700	71,530	13,830	23.5	Fine steely.
1 1/16	One-quarter.	1.20	2	2	56,600	70,600	14,000	24.5	Fine steely.
1 1/8	One-quarter.	1.20	3	3	52,600	65,850	13,190	24.0	Fine steely.
1 3/16	One-quarter.	1.20	2	2	48,000	59,000	11,000	25.0	Fine steely.
1 1/4	One-quarter.	1.20	2	2	58,900	67,400	8,500	14.6	Coarse granulous.
1 5/16	One-quarter.	1.20	2	2	52,400	62,800	10,400	20.0	Fibrous.
1 3/8	One-quarter.	1.20	2	1	54,200	67,200	13,000	24.0	Fibrous.
1 3/8	One-quarter.	1.20	1	..	58,400	67,200	8,800	15.0	Coarse fibre.
1 7/16	One-quarter.	1.20	2	2	46,900	54,500	7,600	16.0	Coarse granulous.
1 7/16	One-quarter.	1.20	2	2	55,450	65,400	9,950	18.0	Gray fibre.
1 1/2	One-half.	1.25	2	2	54,300	66,000	11,700	21.0	Gray fibre.
1 9/16	One-half.	1.25	2	1	58,400	69,700	11,300	19.0	Gray fibre.
1 5/8	One-half.	1.25	2	1	51,500	64,900	13,400	26.	Coarse granulous.
1 3/4	One-half.	1.25	2	1	50,000	62,400	11,500	22.	Coarse granulous.
1 7/8	One-half.	1.25	2	1	44,000	58,500	9,500	19.	Coarse granulous.
1 7/8	One-half.	1.25	2	1	48,200	56,900	8,700	18.	Coarse granulous.

These results made it evident that the government had *not* received iron of such great tensile strength as was supposed; and this was made more certain by the results procured subsequently by comparative tests upon several of the irons which make up our records. These are here given. One groove-test was made upon each size.

Comparison of Results obtained from Cylindrical and from Grooved Test-Pieces. Irons C, B, J, F, L, E.

Iron.		Dimensions of Test-Piece.		No. of Tests.	Ultimate Strength per Square Inch.		Grooves exceed Cylinders by —		Remarks.
Name.	Diameter of Bar.	Diameter.	Length.		Groove.	Cylinder.	Pounds.	Per Cent.	
	In.	In.	In.		Pounds.	Pounds.			
C	1 3/16.	.864	1.25	2	54,800	47,885	6,915	14.5	Strong and tough.
C	1 3/4.	.864	1.20	2	57,700	48,600	9,100	10.8	Hard and coarse.
C	1 5/8.	.564	1.30	2	58,900	56,000	2,900	5	Hard and coarse.
C	1 1/2.	.564	1.20	2	58,300	52,000	6,300	12.1	Hard and coarse.
C	1 7/16.	.564	1.25	2	59,100	45,800	13,300	20	Strong and tough.
B	1 5/16.	.800	1.30	2	67,000	51,900	15,100	29	Strong, good stock.
B	1 1/16.	.800	1.30	2	65,650	53,600	12,050	22.5	Not enough work.
J	1 3/4.	.800	1.30	2	57,300	50,350	6,950	14	Irregular.
J	1 5/8.	.640	1.40	2	62,200	50,300	11,900	24	Irregular.
F	1 3/4.	.800	1.20	2	61,900	50,130	11,770	23.5	Soft and ductile.
F	1 1/4.	.564	1.30	2	60,520	50,400	10,120	20	Soft and ductile.
L	1 3/16.	.800	1.35	2	75,250	58,390	16,860	29	Steel.
L	1 3/4.	.564	1.37	2	74,400	59,290	15,110	25	Steel.
L	1 1/4.	.670	1.35	2	94,400	75,233	19,167	25	Steel.
L	1 1/2.	....	....	1	......	74,600	......	26.5	Steel.
L	1 7/16.	....	....	2	80,000	66,500	13,500	20	Steel.
E	1 3/4.	.800	1.30	2	59,520	50,080	9,440	18	Tough and strong.
E	1 1/2.	.564	1.30	2	61,060	50,000	11,060	21	Tough and strong.

It is to be noticed that the difference between the results obtained by the two methods is greater in pure refined iron than it is in coarse material. A single experiment, made with a test-piece of each form upon cast-iron, confirmed this view: the difference of results was less than one per cent, and the cylinder proved that much the stronger.

A series of experiments was undertaken for the express purpose of enabling us to decide upon the correct form and proportions necessary in the test-pieces to insure correct results. The first of this series was made upon eighteen test-pieces turned from a 2″ bar of a remarkably pure, refined, and uniform iron (K).

No. 1 of this series was 10″ long; and the length decreased upon each successive number, until, at 18, the groove-form was reached. The diameters were nearly constant, except in two cases where seams encountered made it necessary to turn away more iron. The results are given in the following table:—

Iron K.

Number.	Original Length.	Per Cent of Elongation.	Per Cent of Contraction of Area.	Stress per Square Inch when Piece began to Stretch.	Breaking Stress per Square Inch.	Remarks.
	Inches.			Pounds.	Pounds.	
1	10	23.1	38.2	29,678	54,888	Slight seam.
2	9½	24.3	36.5	28,011	55,288	
3	9	21.5	31.1	29,345	55,355	
4	8½	22	31.2	29,345	55,622	
5	7½	25	39.9	30,840	54,890	Slight seam.
6	7	25.8	38.6	30,412	55,488	
7	6½	22.1	40.0	28,562	51,800	Bad seam.
8	6	22.3	34.7	30,600	55,418	
9	5½	25.4	39.3	29,475	55,333	
10	5	21.2	32.2	29,278	55,887	Slight seam.
11	4	25.7	37.4	29,705	55,532	
12	3½	26.7	36.6	31,817	55,482	
13	3	27	38.3	31,123	56,190	
14	2	27	36.2	33,428	56,428	Seamy.
15	1½	26	34.0	42,249	57,096	Seamy.
16	1	37	34.3	34,288	58,933	
17	½	30	37.0	57,565	59,388	Seamy.
18	Groove.	....	20.6	45,442	71,300	

Nos. 13 and 18 of the preceding table are reproduced in the following illustration:—

Fig. 1 being No. 18 of the table, and Fig. 2 No. 13;

In Fig. 1, the length $a\,b$ was 3″, the diameter, $c\,c$, .976″.

In Fig. 2, the length $a\,b$ was 3″, the diameter, $c\,c$, .970″.

The pieces were nearly the same in dimensions; yet the stress at which No. 13 broke, reduced to the square inch, was over fifteen thousand pounds less than that required to break No. 18. This difference would be very great in estimating the entire strength of the bar from the results of the two pieces. Were those from No. 18 correct, the bar would be equal to a strain of *one hundred tons;* while No. 13 shows that less than *seventy-nine* tons would tear it asunder.

By the table, we see that the piece No. 13 gave higher results than those which were longer; the average tensile strength developed by Nos. 2, 3, 4, 6, 9, 10, 11, and 12 being 55,488 pounds per square inch, while No. 13 gives 56,190 pounds,—an excess of 751 pounds,— thus suggesting that the length of this piece, viz.,

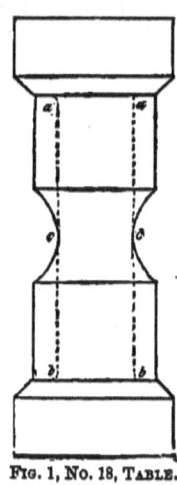
Fig. 1, No. 18, Table.

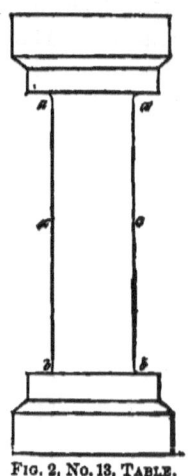
Fig. 2, No. 13, Table.

three inches, was not sufficient to insure correct results.

No. 12 gives a result much closer to the averages, as do Nos. 11 and 10.

Assuming that the proper length should be a certain percentage of the diameter, we find No. 13, which is less than four diameters in length, is not long enough; No. 12, of about four diameters, gives correct results.

The preceding tests in this investigation having been made upon iron with considerable tensile strength, it was thought advisable to make one more experiment with a bar of very soft and ductile iron.

A two-inch bar was selected, which, although of low tensile strength, was very tough and ductile.

From this nine test-pieces were turned, of lengths from eight inches down, to the groove-form, each successive piece being nearly one inch shorter than its predecessor, and all being nearly of uniform diameter. They were tested with the following results: —

Iron D.

No.	Diameter.		Original Length.	Reduction of Area.	Per Cent Elonga- tion.	First Stretch per Square Inch.	Ultimate Stress per Square Inch.
	Original.	Fractured.					
	Inches.	Inches.	Inches.	Per Cent.		Pounds.	Pounds.
1	1.000	.693	8	52	28	28,019	45,800
2	.999	.675	7	54.3	29.8	30,000	45,930
3	1.000	.704	5.82	50.3	20.9	26,700	45,995
4	.999	.700	4.90	50.9	31	28,060	45,768
5	.998	.683	3.95	53.1	35	26,588	46,561
6	1.000	.705	2.98	50.3	36.1	......	46,759
7	1.001	.700	1.98	51	40.4	28,000	46,734
8	1.000	.718	.975	48.4	45.2	28,200	47,033
9	.985	.897	Groove.	17	....	48,000	61,023

The results indicate that with iron of this character a length equal to four diameters is not quite sufficient to insure accurate results.

No. 5, which was nearly four diameters in length, gave a tensile strength greater by 689 pounds per square inch than was developed by Nos. 1, 2, 3, and 4, which were very uniform; No. 4 being five diameters in length, and *long enough*. No. 6, of three diameters, gave still higher results; and when the groove-form was reached there was a sudden rise of over 13,000 pounds, a difference equal to 33 per cent of the actual strength.

In conclusion, our results lead us to the decision, that, in testing iron, no test-piece should be less than one-half inch in diameter, as inaccuracy is more probable with a small than with a large piece, and the errors are more increased by reduction to the square inch; that the length should not be less than four times the diameter in any case; and that, with soft ductile metal, five or six diameters would be preferable.

These rules hold good in testing steel also, according to a number of results, which have been submitted to the committee, of tests made upon American Bessemer rail steel; which results are confirmed by those obtained by Col. Wilmot at the Woolwich Arsenal, made also upon Bessemer steel, which we quote as follows: —

Material, Bessemer steel; test-pieces of one square inch area.

	TENSILE STRENGTH.	POUNDS PER SQUARE INCH.
By groove form:	Highest	162,974
	Lowest	136,490
	Average	153,677
By cylinder:	Highest	123,165
	Lowest	103,255
	Average	114,460

The grooved thus exceeding the cylinder form, 32 to 34 per cent.

PART II. — COMPARATIVE STRENGTH OF BARS IN THEIR NORMAL CONDITION, AND AS REDUCED BY TURNING AWAY THE SKIN AND ADJACENT IRON.

A few tests were made by tension; for the double purpose of ascertaining if the strength per square inch of iron bars with or without the skin is the same, and to compare the results obtained by the two testing-machines A and B. The following tables show some of the results: —

Consolidation of Results from 226 Tests by Tension upon Test-Pieces, with and without Skin, showing Preponderance of Strength in Favor of the Bar in Normal Condition.

TESTING-MACHINE A.

Iron.	Size of Bar.	No. of Tests.		Tensile Strength per Square Inch.		Excess of Strength.	
		Rough.	Turned.	Rough.	Turned.	Rough over Turned.	Turned over Rough.
	Inches.			Pounds.	Pounds.	Pounds.	Pounds.
D	1¾	1	1	51,499	51,895	....	396
D	1⅝	1	1	51,127	50,383	744	....
D	1½	1	1	52,156	53,347	....	1,191
D	1¼	1	1	51,275	51,271	4	....
C	2	1	1	49,678	49,735	33	....
C	1⅞	1	1	49,095	48,726	369	....
C	1 13/16	1	1	49,512	51,367	145	....
C	1¾	1	1	51,233	49,419	1,814	....
E	1⅞	1	1	51,739	49,044	2,695	....
E	1¾	1	1	51,606	51,740	....	134
E	1⅝	1	1	51,944	50,844	1,100	....
E	1½	1	1	55,411	55,409	2	....
E	1⅜	1	1	52,255	51,843	412	....
E	1¼	1	1	53,894	53,309	585	....
E	1⅛	1	1	53,098	53,497	....	399
Hammered .	1¼	1	1	52,570	52,424	146	....
Hammered .	1⅝	1	1	56,818	54,143	2,675	....
Hammered .	1½	2	2	57,280	55,021	2,259	....
Hammered .	1⅛	1	1	55,542	55,805	....	263
F	1	5	1	52,819	52,810	9	....
F	1⅛	5	1	52,267	51,675	592	....
F	1¼	5	1	52,620	51,949	671	....
F	1⅜	5	1	52,537	50,403	2,134	....
F	1½	5	1	51,456	50,799	657	....
F	1⅝	5	1	50,970	49,605	1,365	....
F	1¾	5	1	49,738	50,201	....	463
F	1⅞	5	1	49,061	49,682	....	621
F	2	5	1	47,569	48,170	....	601
F	2¼	2	2	48,505	49,164	....	659
F	2⅜	2	2	47,344	48,475	....	1,131
		69	33				

COMPARATIVE STRENGTH OF ROUGH AND TURNED BARS.

TESTING-MACHINE B.

Iron.	Size of Bar.	No. of Tests.		Tensile Strength per Square Inch.		Excess of Strength.	
		Rough.	Turned.	Rough.	Turned.	Rough over Turned.	Turned over Rough.
	Inches.			Pounds.	Pounds.	Pounds.	Pounds.
C	1¼	4	3	52,949	52,796	153	....
C	1	3	3	54,076	52,475	1,601	....
C	¾	6	5	55,725	55,311	414	....
C	⅝	8	6	57,846	62,813	....	4,967
D	1	6	4	53,400	52,408	992	....
K	1	3	3	62,269	60,536	1,733	....
K	1	4	3	61,945	62,156	....	211
Contract iron,	⅞	3	4	60,466	59,696	770	....
F, first lot .	1	4	4	52,155	51,547	608	....
F, first lot .	1	3	3	52,645	51,540	1,105	....
F, first lot .	¾	6	5	57,257	57,668	....	411
F, first lot .	⅝	6	5	55,644	54,964	680	....
F, third lot .	½	3	1	50,716	50,374	342	....
	⅜	3	1	51,969	50,276	693	....
	⅜	3	1	52,032	51,431	601	....
	¼	3	1	53,755	52,775	980	....
	⅛	3	1	......	......	....	....
		71	53				

In case of the half-inch bars of iron C, of which the turned so greatly exceeded the rough in strength, there is some reason to suspect that a piece of the bar of iron K was by mistake substituted for that of C. In case of iron K, where the turned exceeded the rough bar, the threads of the latter stripped.

The accumulated evidence indicates that the strength of the skin of the bar is greater in proportion to its area than that of the rest of the bar.

In making the foregoing tests, we find that in sixteen comparative tests of small bars by testing-machine B, and in thirty comparative tests upon larger bars by testing-machine A, making forty-six in all, in thirteen cases of the former and twenty of the latter, thirty-three, or over 72 per cent, the excess of strength occurred with bars in their normal condition.

With iron F, which was so uniform in its structure that any peculiarity which manifested itself by any particular test seemed to indicate a possible law, we find that, with the bars which received the most work, viz., from 1″ to 1⅛″ inclusive, the rough bars were stronger than the turned; above 1⅛″ the more slightly-worked sizes reversed the proportion. If this result can be accepted as indicative, it would be wise, in estimating the entire strength of a large bar by the data afforded by the test of a cylinder turned from its centre, to, as has already been said, consider it probable that an over-estimate would be made. For instance, the strength of the 2¼″ bar was 192,861 pounds by actual test of the entire bar; by test of turned bar, 195,481 pounds; by test of cylinder, 195,981 pounds; showing a possible over-estimate of 3,120 pounds by use of cylinder turned from the core.

SECTION III.

Tests of Bars by Impact; showing Action of Various Types of Iron under Sudden Strains.

THE tests by which we have ascertained the powers of the various irons of the series to resist steady tensional strains, applied in the direction of the fibre, and when manufactured into links, have furnished us with no data by which their relative powers to resist sudden strains, applied transversely, could be judged. As cables are more frequently broken by strains of this nature than by all other causes combined, it was considered to be absolutely necessary that the series should be subjected to such tests as would develop their relative values in this respect before we could express an opinion as to which of the varying characteristics, as developed by tension alone, indicated that the iron in which they existed could be considered as in every way suitable for the manufacture of cables.

Having no apparatus by which such tests could be made, one was devised by the chairman of the committee, by the use of which we were enabled to form a fair judgment as to the *comparative* values of the irons when subjected to shocks.

The following is a description of this machine, which was known as the "impact hammer:"—

The Impact Hammer.— A cast-iron hammer having a wedge-shaped impact surface upon its lower side is made to transverse two perpendicular iron rods of say $2\frac{1}{2}$ inches diameter and from

30 to 50 feet in length, which pass through holes in the body of the hammer. The hammer may be of any weight, a convenient one being 100 pounds. A traveller of wood or metal, fitted with a pair of hooks which can be opened or closed by pulling up a cord attached to them, is placed upon the rods above the hammer. At the foot of the rods, they passing through it, is fitted a cast-iron block with a cylindrical opening eight inches in diameter. The specimen of iron to be tested is placed across this circular hole, the hammer resting upon the box which surrounds the anvil and supported by a chock, to prevent accidents. A common purchase, through which a hoisting-rope is led to the windlass, is secured to the portion of the framework. At the side of one of the rods an upright, marked plainly in feet and inches, is secured.

To use the machine, the hammer is hoisted to the desired height, the lower edge of the hammer being brought in line with the figure on the measuring-rod. When at the proper height, the tripping-line is pulled, opening the hooks, and releasing the hammer, which falls, striking the specimen in the centre a blow whose force can be measured, and which is dependent upon the force of gravity at the location, and slightly diminished by friction.

METHOD OF TESTING BY IMPACT.

Our method of testing by this machine was this: Test-pieces, not less than twelve diameters in length, were placed across the hole through the anvil, the centres being directly under the edge of the wedge-shaped hammer, which was raised to various heights, and allowed to drop upon them.

Bars of some irons which were tested by this method could, while in their normal condition, the skin being in no manner nicked or weakened, be broken by two blows of less than three thousand foot-pounds force; with other irons it was necessary to weaken them by a circular score $\frac{1}{32}$ of an inch deep, that we might succeed in breaking the test-piece, it not being convenient to use a hammer over one hundred pounds weight.

which could be hoisted but thirty feet. This cut through the skin reduced the bar's power to resist, in the same manner that it is reduced by the ordinary method of nicking with a cold-chisel, and the blows of the hammer were of the same nature as those given by sledge-hammers; but with this machine the force of the blow could be regulated and known, and the weakening produced by the cuts made uniform.

The wedge-shaped portion of the hammer permitted a bar to bend to an angle of 120.°

Through the data collected by the test, by this method, of a large number of bars of various irons differing widely in character, we were able to detect the existence of a connecting link, and partially trace its course, between the characteristics displayed under tension, and those produced by impact.

Iron with high tensile strength generally proved to be possessed of but comparatively low resilience; it would break under the blows with but slight deflection, and leave a fractured surface, smooth as though the bar had been cut in two by a sharp knife, the ends of the fibres showing, like steel, a fine, slightly granulous surface.

Iron of coarse, slightly-worked character would have an equally smooth and bright surface, but the coarse, granulous appearance of the cut fibres denoted how slightly they had been affected by the rolls.

Iron with a high elastic limit would resist the first blow, with but little injury or deflection; but, the deflection once started by subsequent blows, it would yield more at each than would other irons with a lower limit, which were more affected by the first blow. Some irons would, after having been weakened by the circular cut through the skin, resist, with slight injury, blows which would break in two bars of the same size of other irons which had not been so weakened.

There are many irons, valuable for many purposes, which would not yield good results under this form of test; but, however valuable for other purposes, the material which proves brittle under test cannot be expected, when made into cable, and subjected to strains of a similar nature, to prove equal to its tasks.

Iron which is materially weakened by a repetition of slight, sudden strains, none of which produce perceptible injury, but which do so injure it that eventually a strain no greater, and perhaps much less, than those previously encountered, will destroy it, is not suitable for cable. Iron whose entire strength depends upon its remaining perfectly free from abrasion, or slight cracks, is not suitable for cables. Our tests by impact revealed that large quantities of iron possessing the above defects had been accumulated by the government, all having passed satisfactorily the examinations, which consisted of tension tests made upon test-pieces of erroneous proportions. Much of this iron was of good material; but the low price at which it had to be supplied, in order that the *lowest bidder* should, as the law directed, receive the contract, had necessitated, that, in order to make it cheap enough, but very little work should be expended upon it.

Our experiments demonstrated not only its want of value in its present state, but also that by thorough work it could be vastly improved; and when, in addition to this work, material of no greater cost, but possessing qualities that the coarse chain-iron lacked, was added, we found that most valuable iron, capable of resisting all strains, was produced.

An example of such a transformation will be described: The material selected was taken from the pile of $2\frac{3}{16}''$ chain-iron, and was probably as inferior a bar of iron as could be found in the pile, or in our markets, there being in the stock of chain-iron, however, a great many equally poor.

These bolts, each over 26″ long, were thoroughly tested. Several which had not been weakened by a score were broken square in two by a single blow of the hammer dropped twenty-five to thirty feet; others, having been struck from ten to twenty times by the hammer, from a height of eight or ten feet, and showing no injury or deflection, would, upon receiving another blow of no greater force, break in two; other bars, scored as has been described, would break in two at single blows of from one to three feet drop.

In all cases, the appearance of the fracture was the same, and would be described as "bright, coarse, granulous."

Iron from this lot, having been first thoroughly re-worked, was piled with alternate layers of *old boiler-iron*, and hammered into a bloom, from which a bar of 2" diameter was swaged. This was cut into pieces 24" long, and the pieces were scored in two places, 8" apart, and then tested as was the original bar, except that each drop of the hammer was from a height of *thirty feet*. The first score received ten such blows before it was entirely torn in two, and the fractured surface appeared fibrous.

The extreme difference between the appearance of fractures made upon the same material (and it of great resisting powers), by different degrees of the same force, indicates that it is unsafe, even for an expert, to attempt to give evidence as to the character of the material from which a bridge, axle, or cable, that has been accidentally broken, was made, unless he knows just *how* it was broken. To render a judgment upon this point, a person must not only be an expert, but he must know by what character and amount of force the fracture was produced.

The fractures illustrated in the frontispiece, Fig. 2, supply evidence of this fact. The three were made by impact upon the same bar (of iron A, 1¼" diameter) which was scored in three places, eight inches apart. At *a* the score was slight, and the piece was torn in two by repeated light blows.

At *b* the score was the same; but, after the bar had been broken half in two by light blows, one heavy one was given, which *cut* in two the remainder.

At *c* the score was deep, and one heavy blow did the work: *a* would be described as "all fibrous," *b* as "half granulous and half fibrous," *c* as "bright granulous."

Irons F, Fx, O, D, H, G, Px, and some of the bars of B, C, and P, resemble more or less in their characteristics the iron shown in this plate.

BARKING.

A peculiar phenomenon occurred with irons of a certain type, during the test by impact, which was given the shop name of "barking." The illustration in frontispiece, Fig. 1, will give a clearer idea than description can of this phenomenon. This occurred only in tests of very tough, ductile iron which had been thoroughly worked, and which required several repetitions of the blows to break in two.

As the deflection caused by each successive blow increased, the transverse crack at the lower part of the test-piece widened, and the surface iron became detached, and stood open like a detached bark. A tough gray ligature with splintered surface connected the two ends, and a finger could be thrust under the skin on either side.

Several photographs were made of instances of this action; it being deemed peculiar to most excellent iron, occurring only with A, C, F, Fx, and O.

CRYSTALLIZATION.

The question as to whether crystallization can be produced in iron by stress, or by repetition of stress with alternations of rest, or by vibration, has been much discussed, and very opposite views are entertained by experts.

We have met but with one unmistakable instance of crystallization which was probably produced by alternations of severe stress, sudden strains, recoils, and rest.

The connecting-rod of the chain-prover was five inches in diameter, and had been in use for forty years, and had, during this period, been frequently subjected to stress up to 250,000 pounds, with recoils produced by rupture of test pieces.

It was carefully made in the anchor-shop, being hammered from the best quality of wrought-iron scrap. It is not probable than any section of it, if broken when first made, would have displayed crystalline structure; but, while we were testing, it parted one day at less than 200,000 pounds stress, and the surface of the fractured ends showed well-defined crystallization, the facets being large and bright as mica. The ends having become injured by rust, the bar was again broken by impact at a point distant over a foot from the first fracture, and the same appearance was found. The original of this fracture is now in the cabinet of Stevens Institute of Technology.

Impact Tests.

The records of tests by impact begin with the history of an examination made upon the contract chain-iron in store, made by the chairman of these committees, acting under the instructions of the Navy Department, with the object of ascertaining the character of the iron on hand, and the effect of thorough re-working upon such as was found unsuitable for cables.

This iron was stowed in piles classified by diameters. Most of it had been received during the war from such contractors as had bid lowest, and its origin beyond this point was unknown: its general character, as found by this examination, was worthless in its present state. The results of the experiments in re-working, and in combining it with scrap-iron of a superior quality, were such that the iron produced was pronounced by the Chief of the Bureau of Steam Engineering as "at least equal, if not superior, to the best commercial iron, at less cost."

[The original report contains the records of about a thousand impact tests. From these the abridger has selected the records of irons F and M, as showing the variation of resistance to impact between a soft, ductile iron, and a hard, brittle iron.]

Record of Tests by Impact.

IRON F. — UNSCORED.

Number of Test.	Diameter.	Force and Effect of Blows.																Remarks.	
		First.		Second.		Third.		Fourth.		Fifth.		Sixth.		Seventh.		Eighth.			
		Force, Foot-pounds.	Effect and Deflection.	Force, Foot-pounds.	Effect and Deflection.	Force, Foot-pounds.	Effect and Deflection.	Force, Foot-pounds.	Effect and Deflection.	Force, Foot-pounds.	Effect and Deflection.	Force, Foot-pounds.	Effect and Deflection.	Force, Foot-pounds.	Effect and Deflection.	Force, Foot-pounds.	Effect and Deflection.		
1	2″	3,000	22	3,000	35	3,000	48	3,000	60	3,000	79	3,000	85	3,000	96	3,000	109	Closed down under steam hammer without injury.	
2	1⅞	3,000	27	3,000	43	3,000	62	3,000	78	3,000	100	3,000	100	....	..	....	...	Closed down under steam hammer without injury.	
3	1¾	3,000	34	3,000	60	3,000	72	3,000	95	3,000	110	....	...	....	..	....	...	Closed down under steam hammer without injury.	
4	1⅝	3,000	39	3,000	64	3,000	90	3,000	111	....	...	....	...	....	..	....	...	Closed down under steam hammer; crack across butt.	
5	1½	3,000	46	3,000	82	3,000	107	....	...	....	...	....	...	....	..	....	...	Closed down under steam hammer; crack across butt.	
6	1⅜	3,000	60	3,000	97	3,000	118	....	...	....	...	....	...	....	..	....	...	Closed down under steam hammer without injury.	
7	1¼	3,000	76	3,000	110	....	...	....	...	....	...	....	...	....	..	....	...	Closed down under steam hammer without injury.	
8	1⅛	3,000	103	....	....	....	...	....	...	....	...	....	...	....	..	....	...	Closed down under steam hammer without injury.	
9	1	3,000	112	....	....	....	...	....	...	....	...	....	...	....	..	....	...	Closed down under steam hammer without injury.	

SCORED.

10	2	3,000	S.C. 18	3,000	B.C. 31	3,000	+45	3,000	+62	3,000	+90	3,000	110½ F	....	..	....	...	Closed to face of hammer.	
11	1⅞	3,000	C. 23	3,000	½F	....	...	....	...	....	...	....	.....	....	..	....	...	Gray fibre, end hanging.	
12	1¾	3,000	C. 39	3,000	½F	....	...	....	...	....	...	....	.....	....	..	....	...	Gray fibre, broken in two.	
13	1⅝	3,000	F.	....	......	....	...	....	...	....	...	....	.....	....	..	....	...	Gray fibre, broken in two.	
14	1½	2,500	C. 27	2,000	B.C. 55	2,000	½F.	....	...	....	...	....	.....	....	..	....	...	Gray fibre, broken in two.	All showed long, fibrous structure.
15	1⅜	2,500	90 F.	....	......	....	...	....	...	....	...	....	.....	....	..	....	...	Gray fibre, broken in two.	
16	1¼	2,200	F.	....	......	....	...	....	...	....	...	....	.....	....	..	....	...	Gray fibre, broken in two.	
17	1⅛	1,800	F.	....	......	....	...	....	...	....	...	....	.....	....	..	....	...	Gray fibre, broken in two.	
18	1	1,000	F.	....	......	....	...	....	...	....	...	....	.....	....	..	....	...	Gray fibre, broken in two.	

TESTS OF BARS BY IMPACT. 39

IRON M. — UNSCORED.

Number of Test.	Diameter.	Force and Effect of Blows.						Remarks.
		First.		Second.		Third.		
		Force, Foot-pounds.	Effect and Deflection.	Force, Foot-pounds.	Effect and Deflection.	Force, Foot-pounds.	Effect and Deflection.	
1	2¼"	3,000	□	....	..	....	..	All bright granulous.
2	2¼	2,500	□	....	..	....	..	All bright granulous.
3	2	2,500	□	....	..	....	..	All bright granulous.
4	2	2,000	C	500	□	....	..	All bright granulous.
5	1⅞	2,000	C	1,000	□	....	..	90 per cent bright granulous.
6	1⅞	2,200	F	....	..	....	..	90 per cent bright granulous.
7	1¾	2,000	□	....	..	....	..	80 per cent bright; the rest dark and dull.
8	1¾	1,500	C	500	□	....	..	
9	1¾	1,500	C	300	F	....	..	80 per cent bright; the rest dull, short fibre.
10	1⅝	1,600	□	....	..	....	..	
11	1½	1,700	□	....	..	....	..	About equally mixed, dark short fibre, and bright granulous.
12	1½	1,000	C	1,000	+	600	F	
13	1⅜	1,200	□	....	..	....	..	All bright granulous; very short.
14	1⅜	1,000	□	....	..	....	..	90 per cent bright granulous; very short.
15	1⅜	800	□	....	..	....	..	Bright granulous; very short.
16	1⅜	600	F	....	..	....	..	
17	1⅜	500	C	300	F	....	..	90 per cent bright; the rest dull fibre on one side.
18	1⅜	400	C	400	+	400	F	90 per cent bright granulous.
19	1⅜	600	□	....	..	....	..	Mixed dull fibre and bright granulous.
20	1⅜	500	T	....	..	....	..	End just hanging on by small bit of fibre; the rest bright granulous.

Explanation of Symbols used in the above Tables.

The figures under "effect and deflection" are deflections in degrees, from horizontal.
"S.C.," a slight crack in which a needle-point could be inserted, and
"C.," a crack wide and deep enough to insert the edge of a knife.
"+," an increase in the opening, but not enough to term
"B.C.," a bad crack.
"F.," a fracture in which the ends are torn apart, leaving long, jagged splinters.
"IF.," an incomplete fracture of the same nature, the ends still remaining connected.
"□," a short square break, with little or no deflection, the fractured surfaces showing smooth as if cut in two.
"Closed to hammer," the test-piece is bent to from 110° to 120°, and in contact with the face of the wedge of the hammer.
"Closed down," the piece has been still further closed under the steam hammer, until the sides are in contact the whole length.

SECTION IV.

A Paper describing a Series of Experiments to determine Facts in regard to the Operation of the Law called the Elevation of the Limit of Stress.

THE discovery that wrought-iron, after having been subjected to a steady stress up to the point of its ultimate strength, would, if then released from stress and permitted to rest, experience an elevation in both its elastic and tensile limit, was made by Professor Robert H. Thurston in November, 1873, and by the chairman of these committees a short time afterward, while carrying on an investigation by tension, Professor Thurston having made his discovery by torsion tests. The discoveries were entirely independent, neither experimenter having any knowledge of the other's work.

As, at the beginning of the series of tests incorporated in this report, but little data had been obtained as to the operation of this new law, it was thought worth while, while making investigations in regard to chain-iron, to utilize at slight expense many of the test-pieces, in investigating its action. By bringing a test-piece to the tensile limit, all data as to its strength are obtained; and by carrying the test to rupture, we gain simply the dimensions after rupture, and means to reduce the strength, &c., to those measurements.

We therefore released a number of test-pieces from stress, when the tensile limit was reached, and, preserving them for various periods, eventually broke them, with results as given in the following paper: —

ELEVATION OF THE LIMIT OF THE STRESS.

Experiments Nos. 1 to 10.

Twelve test-pieces which had been strained to the point of "tensile limit" while testing irons C, D, and K, were permitted to rest free from strain for from twenty-four to thirty hours, then broken with results as follows: —

No. 1. Iron C, 2"; strength second day over that at first test, 3,357 pounds per square inch, or 6.6 per cent.

No. 2. Iron C, $1\frac{7}{8}$"; strength second day over that at first test, 2,238 pounds per square inch, or 4.4 per cent.

No. 3. Iron C, $1\frac{1}{4}$"; strength second day over that at first test, 7,506 pounds per square inch, or 15.1 per cent.

No. 4. Iron C, $1\frac{1}{8}$"; strength second day over that at first test, 8,560 pounds per square inch, or 17 per cent.

No. 5. Iron D, 2"; strength second day over that at first test, 952 pounds per square inch, or 2 per cent.

No. 6. Iron D, $1\frac{7}{8}$"; strength second day over that at first test, 7,354 pounds per square inch, or 15.7 per cent.

No. 7. Iron D, $1\frac{3}{4}$"; strength second day over that at first test, 7,773 pounds per square inch, or 16.1 per cent.

No. 8. Iron D, $1\frac{5}{8}$"; strength second day over that at first test, 8,605 pounds per square inch, or 16.7 per cent.

No. 9. Iron D, $1\frac{1}{2}$"; strength second day over that at first test, 6,904 pounds per square inch, or 14.1 per cent.

No. 10. Iron D, $1\frac{1}{4}$"; strength second day over that at first test, 8,325 pounds per square inch, or 16.3 per cent.

No. 11. Iron K, $1\frac{1}{4}$"; strength second day over that at first test, 4,203 pounds per square inch, or 8.2 per cent.

No. 12. Iron K, 1"; strength second day over that at first test, 5,040 pounds per square inch, or 8.8 per cent.

Nos. 11 and 12 were of a fine, strong iron, with considerable carbon, breaking with a steel-like fracture: the remainder were all from tough, fibrous iron. The indications were that the latter type of iron gained the most by the rest. While testing the foregoing pieces, the stress which produced the first perceptible elongation (about .002 of an inch) was observed; and on the first test this stress was from 61 to 70, averaging about 65 per cent of the ultimate strength. Upon testing them the second time, the stress which produced first stretch was nearly identical with the ultimate strength.

Second Experiment.— Forty-two test-pieces of iron F, which was of remarkably uniform structure, were, after having been strained to "tensile limit," allowed to rest for periods varying from one *minute* to *six months*, when they were re-tested with results as per table.

Elevation of the Limit of Stress. Iron F. Abstract from Detail of Tests.

	PER CENT.	TESTS.
Average gain in less than one hour	1.1	5
Average gain in less than eight and over one hour,	3.8	8
Average gain in three days	16.2	10
Average gain in eight days	17.8	2
Average gain in over eight and less than forty-three days	15.3	5
Average gain in six months	17.9	12
		42

The elongation was irregular; that of those broken at first stress and of those after six months' rest coinciding at 29 per cent, while intermediates varied from 27.5 per cent to 30 per cent.

Having failed to procure data as to the effect of rest after strain, for periods between eight hours and three days, it was resolved to fill the hiatus with a series made upon iron D, which resembled iron F, except in possessing somewhat greater tenacity when tested as an entire bar.

Seven test-pieces were brought to tensile limit upon one day, and broken after twenty-four hours of rest, with an average gain of 15.4 per cent. This is but slightly below that of the pieces of iron F rested three days (16.2 per cent); and we may consider that at the end of one day the result is, with very ductile irons, practically accomplished.

Reduction of Strength between the Ultimate reached, and Breaking-point.

Six of the forty-two pieces were, after reaching the tensile limit, on the second test, still further tested thus: The lever having fallen, weights were removed until a balance took place, which balance was maintained by removal of weights while the crank was turned without cessation, but slowly; and the specimens finally ruptured at strains considerably less than the original strength, thus:—

Interval between First and Second Tests.	Original Strength.	Strength at Rupture.	Loss.	
			Pounds.	Per Cent.
	Pounds.	Pounds.		
1 hour	49,345	42,952	6,393	12.9
2 hours	49,358	43,049	6,309	12.9
3 "	49,401	42,271	7,130	14.4
4 "	49,206	42,364	6,842	13.9
5 "	50,257	42,914	7,343	14.5
6 "	50,313	43,121	7,192	14.2
Average	.....	.....	6,868	13.8

Percentage of Change of Form at Tensile Limit to that at Fracture.

At tensile limit the average reduction of area which had taken place was equal to 53 per cent of that at rupture, and the average percentage of elongation was 80 per cent.

The average of the same percentages upon the twenty-three pieces broken by single continued strain was, of reduction of area, 49 per cent; of elongation, 78 per cent: from which averages we deduce, that, at the instant of ceasing to resist an increase of stress, the reduction of area which has taken place is about one-half, and of elongation a little over three-quarters, of that which will have occurred if the metal be further strained to rupture. This, we believe, will not prove true if the metal is ruptured by a sudden strain, by the action of which the fractured dimensions will nearly coincide with those which would have existed at tensile limit had the piece been broken by steady strains. This was indicated by the results of an experiment with an apparatus which we devised, by which we were enabled to apply sudden strains to the specimen.

By means of a pair of spring clamps, a holder was attached to the upper and lower clamps of the dynamometer; and the stress produced by turning the crank, or some indefinite portion of it, was accumulated in the legs of this holder, and at will transferred suddenly to the specimen. The machine was imperfect, its use involved risk of injury to the dynamometer, and we made but one test with it, which was as follows: —

Comparison of Effect of Steady and Sudden Strains upon Change of Form.

Two specimens of nearly the same dimensions were turned from iron E.

No. 1, having diameter .565", length 2.27".

No. 2, having diameter .565", length 2.25".

No. 1 was broken by steady tension, and at tensile limit its diameter was .498", length 2.80". No. 2 was broken by a series of jerks, and its ruptured dimensions were, diameter .496", length 2.87"; the ruptured dimensions of No. 1 being, diameter .407", length 3.00".

Comparison of Elevation of Limit of Stress, upon Irons of differing Characteristics.

The first series of experiments (Nos. 1 to 12) gave indications that the operation of the law was less felt by coarse and brittle irons, and by those of a steely structure, than by those of a more fibrous ductile texture. This was considered to be a point worthy of careful examination, and a series of comparative experiments was made upon test-pieces composed of the three varieties of iron. Thirteen pieces were prepared, five of which were of soft charcoal bloom boiler-iron, five of coarse contract chain-iron, and three of a fine-grained bar of iron K, a very pure iron with high tenacity. These pieces were all made of uniform proportions, and were tested to tensile limit upon the same day. They were then allowed to rest *eighteen hours*, and again tested. Some were broken at this second test; others released from stress at tensile limit, and further tested after varying periods of rest, as per following table, in which Nos. 62 to 66 were of the boiler-iron, 67 to 71 of the contract chain, and 72 to 74 of iron K.

Effect of Uniform Rest upon Irons of widely different Character.

TEST-PIECES RESTED EIGHTEEN HOURS.

Number and Marks.	Ultimate Strength per Square Inch.		Gain in Strength per Square Inch.		Remarks.
	First Strain.	Second Strain.	Pounds.	Per Cent.	
	Pounds.	Pounds.			
62, Boiler iron	48,600	56,500	7,900	16.0	Not broken.
63, "	49,800	57,000	7,200	16.4	Broken. ⎫
64, "	49,800	58,000	9,200	18.4	Broken. ⎬ Average
65, "	48,100	54,400	6,300	13.1	Broken. ⎨ 15.8 per cent.
66, "	48,150	55,550	7,400	15.0	Broken. ⎭
67, Contract chain iron	50,200	54,000	3,800	7.5	Broken.
68, " "	50,250	53,200	2,950	5.8	Not broken. ⎫
69, " "	50,700	55,300	4,600	9.0	Not broken. ⎬ Average
70, " "	49,600	52,900	3,300	6.6	Not broken. ⎨ 6.4 per cent.
71, " "	51,200	52,800	1,600	3.2	Not broken. ⎭
72, Iron K	58,800	64,500	5,700	9.6	Broken. ⎫
73, "	59,000	65,800	6,800	11.5	Broken. ⎬ Average
74, "	56,400	60,600	4,200	7.3	Broken. ⎭ 9.4 per cent.

These experiments confirmed the opinion already formed, and indicate that a bridge, cable, or other structure composed of iron of either of the latter two varieties, will receive comparatively slight benefit from the operation of this law; while ductile, fibrous metal, which possesses greater inherent power to resist sudden strains than does the iron of a coarser nature, although the latter may be better able to resist steady stress, gains in this latter power to a greater extent by the effect of strains already withstood.

46 WROUGHT-IRON AND CHAIN-CABLES.

Supplemental Tests of Nos. 62, 68, 69, 70, and 71, of foregoing Test-Pieces.

No. 62, after having been strained to the tensile limit the second time, was released from stress, and re-tested after *one year's rest*, when its ultimate strength was found to be 59,500 pounds, a total gain of 22 per cent upon the original strength.

No. 68 was rested for 7 hours, 41 hours, and 24 hours, and after each rest repulled to the tensile limit, with results as follows (the first two tests being included for ready comparison): Strength, first strain, 50,250 pounds; rested 18 hours, strength 53,200 pounds; rested 7 hours, strength 54,700 pounds; rested 41 hours, strength 54,500 pounds; rested 24 hours, strength 54,000 pounds.

No. 69. First strain, strength 50,700 pounds; rested 18 hours, strength 55,300 pounds; rested 7 hours, strength 53,150 pounds; rested 41 hours, strength 56,600 pounds; rested 24 hours, strength 54,000 pounds.

No. 70. First strain, strength 49,600 pounds; rested 18 hours, strength 52,900 pounds; rested 8 hours, strength 51,000 pounds; rested 16 hours, strength 54,800 pounds; rested 24 hours, strength 53,000 pounds.

No. 71. First strain, strength 51,200 pounds; rested 18 hours, strength 52,800 pounds; rested 8 hours, strength 54,900 pounds; rested 16 hours, strength 52,750 pounds; rested 24 hours, strength 51,750 pounds.

The four pieces were broken at the strains last given.

Experiments with Two Sets of Test-Pieces: One Set cut from Bars in their Normal Condition, the other from the same Bars after the Latter had been pulled asunder by Tension.

Nineteen bars of various irons were selected, and from each a cylindrical test-piece was prepared: the bars were then fitted with heads, and pulled asunder by tension. Another set of cylinders was prepared by cutting the necessary length from one of the broken ends, about six inches from the point of rupture. Both sets of cylinders were tested, with results as per following table, showing a great gain in strength in all cases when the material could be classed as wrought-iron, but none when it was steel. Hence we infer that excess of carbon deprives iron of the power to gain strength through the action of this law.

Experiments Nos. 75 to 96. — Comparison of Strength of Two Sets of Test-Pieces, the first of which was cut from Bars in their Normal Condition, and the second from the same Bars after the latter had been pulled in Two.

No. of Test.	Size of Bar.	Name of Iron.	Stress required to break the Test-Pieces per Square Inch.		Strength of Second Set over First.	
			First Set.	Second Set.	Pounds.	Per Cent.
	Inch.		Pounds.	Pounds.	Per Sq. Inch.	
75	$1\frac{3}{8}$	K	53,520	72,700	19,180	35.8
76	$1\frac{1}{16}$	K	53,920	71,800	17,880	33.1
77	$1\frac{3}{16}$	C	47,875	63,560	15,685	32.7
78	$1\frac{1}{4}$	C	48,600	65,000	16,400	33.7
79	$1\frac{3}{8}$	C	56,000	73,000	17,000	30.3
80	$1\frac{1}{8}$	C	52,000	67,900	15,900	30.6
81	$1\frac{7}{16}$	C	45,800	63,300	17,500	36
82	$1\frac{3}{16}$	B	51,900	72,000	20,100	38.7
83	$1\frac{1}{16}$	B	53,600	68,700	15,100	28.1
84	$1\frac{3}{8}$	J	50,350	68,400	18,050	35.8
85	$1\frac{3}{8}$	J	50,400	67,700	17,300	34.3
86	$1\frac{1}{4}$	F	50,180	66,400	16,220	32.3
87	$1\frac{1}{4}$	F	50,400	67,200	16,800	33.3
88	$1\frac{1}{4}$	E	50,080	68,000	17,920	35.7
89	$1\frac{1}{8}$	E	50,100	70,100	20,000	39.9
90	$1\frac{3}{16}$	L	58,390	69,200	10,810	18.5
91	$1\frac{1}{4}$	L	59,290	67,160	7,870	13.2
92	$1\frac{1}{4}$	L	75,233	76,600	......	....
93	$1\frac{1}{4}$	L	84,800	......	......	....
94	$1\frac{1}{4}$	L	74,600	72,600	Decrease.	....
95	$1\frac{7}{16}$	L	66,500	......	......	....
96	$1\frac{7}{16}$	L	66,800	73,900	5,250	7.9

The test-pieces from Nos. 75 to 89 inclusive were made from ordinary commercial bar-iron of various degrees of ductility. All show a remarkably great strength, caused by tension upon the entire bars.

The interval of time between the two sets of tests was not noted, but it was several days.

There is no marked difference in the amount of elevation, except upon the test-pieces made from L, which was a weld-steel, although sent to us as chain-iron. With this metal the results were exceedingly irregular, and it was thought advisable to make a few careful tests upon it. Four pieces were therefore prepared from a bar of ⅝″ diameter, which were tested to the tensile limit, and then rested for one hour, one day, one week, and one month, respectively, when they were re-tested with results as follows:—

Experiments Nos. 97 to 100. Material " Iron " L (Weld Steel).

NUMBER.	ORIGINAL DIMENSIONS.		STRENGTH PER SQUARE INCH.		PERIOD OF REST.	GAIN IN STRENGTH.	
	Diameter.	Length.	At first Test.	At second Test.		Pounds.	Per Cent.
	Inches.		Pounds.	Pounds.			
97	.500	2.25	59,078	58,619	1 hour	−459	...
98	.500	2.25	58,569	57,805	1 day	−764	...
99	.406	2.25	59,000	59,653	1 week	+653	1.
100	.501	2.25	59,859	61,694	1 month . . .	+1,834	3.

The entire series of tests by tension upon this metal indicates such irregularity in its strength that the foregoing tests do not possess a positive value; but they *indicate* that there is a great difference between the action of weld-steel and even steely irons, and still greater between it and fibrous iron when examined in reference to the action of this law. We obtain no positive evidence that any increase of strength is caused in steel, by rest after strain.

SECTION V.

THE CABLE.

The information which we have gained by the results of our tests of round bars has its value in determining the characteristics of a suitable cable-iron, but it does not supply us with all that we need.

The cable-link consists of a round bolt, twelve diameters in length, which has been bent into an oval form, and the ends welded together. A stud or stay is introduced between the sides, to prevent closure under stress, and kinking, while the cable is being handled or used.

The tension tests upon the bars show us what strength should exist in each of the sides of the link; and the impact tests give us an idea as to the power of the transverse sections of the ends to resist stress suddenly applied, *if* the process by which the bar is transformed to a link has no power to change the qualities as found in the bars.

This process involves twice reheating and hammering the ends of the bolts, — once to make the scarfs, and once to make the welds, while the butt end of the link has at the same time with the ends been heated once for bending. This forging and re-heating has a tendency to lower the elastic limit and strength of the two ends of the bolt upon which the weld is made; the process of bending affects some irons injuriously; and the comparatively incompressible stud, which prevents closure, alters the nature of the strains.

If none of these causes reduced the strength of a link, and

the single area of each end should be so strengthened by its arched form that it would be equal to the two sides combined, the strength would be just twice that of the bar from which it was made.

A suitable chain-iron is one which will develop in the link form the greatest and most uniform proportion of this two hundred per cent. And the development of a low or irregular proportion indicates that the iron is *not* suitable. The divergence from the two hundred per cent marks the extent to which an iron can be called suitable.

The causes which operate upon all irons to reduce their percentage are, first, the weld; second, the stud. We have tested a large number of chain-links to destruction, and their action under the strain of tension has been carefully noted. We find that the lowest percentages of the bar's strength are developed by those irons which do not permit strong and thorough welding by ordinary processes; and that, in breaking links of all variety of irons, the weld end is generally the weak part of the link; and that with certain types of iron this weakness is so great and of so frequent occurrence that cables made from such iron are very unreliable.

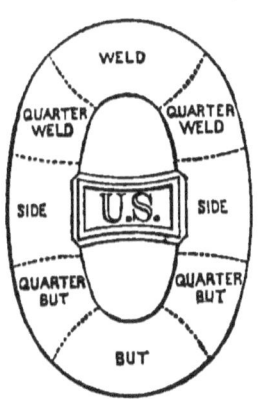

In the rupture of 435 links, 333 of them broke at the weld end, 86 at the butt end, and 16 on the side.

The most ordinary location of the rupture, if we except irons Fx, F, L, M, and Px, was at the quarter of the weld; which rupture is produced by a resolution of the force of direct tension and the resistance opposed by the stud.

The sketch will show the parts of the links designated as quarter weld, &c.

An examination of the records of the strength of links, and of the percentage of the bar's strength developed by the links, will show that all of those links which broke "through the weld" were very weak and irregular in both factors. Hence an iron whose weld is through any cause unreliable is not suitable for cable.

Experiments indicate that we cannot strengthen the link by changing the location of the weld, and our only resource is to select such iron as is least injured by the process of welding.

Among the causes which produce deficiency in welding properties, there are two which produce great tenacity in the bar, viz., chemical peculiarities and excessive work: therefore, when excessive tensile strength is found to exist in a bar as tested by tension, it should be regarded as a probable indication of deficient welding properties. As may be seen by the records of tension and impact compared, high tenacity in the bar frequently indicates a lack of power to resist sudden strains. Therefore, in judging iron by tensile strength alone, it should be considered as more than probable that *the strongest bars will produce the weakest cables*, although there will undoubtedly be in each of such a few links with greater strength than can be developed by irons of less tenacity.

The second cause which tends to prevent the link from developing twice the strength of the bar is the stud.

Our experiments lead us to consider that the opinion which is generally entertained, and which is backed by the most eminent authorities, that the studded link is stronger than the unstudded one made from the same iron, is erroneous, both in principle and in fact.

Rankine, in his "Manual of Machinery" says, "An unstudded chain has about two-thirds of the strength of a studded chain of the same diameter of wire." John Anderson, LL.D., superintendent of machinery to the War Department, Woolwich, in a work published in 1872, says, "It is to be noted, whatever the explanation may be, that the stayed-link chain, when made of the same diameter of iron as the open-link, is stronger than the other in the proportion of 9 to 6. The office of the stud is to prevent the collapse of the link, and thereby intercept the shearing action due to the wedge action of one link within the other."

American authorities coincide with the above opinions, with which, however, we entirely differ. Theoretically it should not be stronger, actually it is weaker, than the open-link.

Theory indicates that when the links are without studs they might stretch until they nipped each other, and then be in the best possible position to resist stress; the sides being parallel and separated but by their own diameter, the ends so closed together that the stress is received and transmitted through bearing surfaces much greater than before the parts had yielded to stress.

Our experience in testing cable links showed us that with all classes of iron this tendency to assume the strongest possible form existed, but in very different degrees; and in this difference we find a possible reason for the different conclusions that have been arrived at by the English experimenters and by ourselves. The English use for chain-cables iron of great tenacity, and the studs to their links are made of malleable iron.

Our experiments have been made both with links of iron of similar character, and with others made from iron with medium and low tenacity, but with great ductility and power of flexure. In all cases we have, however, used the ordinary cast-iron stud.

Experiments made upon iron of a soft ductile type showed that the excess of the strength of the unstudded link over that of the studded ranged from twelve to seventeen per cent, averaging about fifteen per cent, of the strength of the studded links; while with links made of iron of a coarse, hard type the excess of strength was about five per cent, as shown by the following tests.

EXPERIMENTS UPON COMPARATIVE STRENGTH OF STUDDED AND UNSTUDDED LINKS MADE FROM SOFT DUCTILE IRONS (C AND F); DIAMETER OF IRON, $1\frac{1}{8}''$.

The links were arranged in seven sections, of three links each; of which the centre link was in each case an open one, and the two end links (E L) were connected to the proving-bar by means of links of considerably greater diameter ($1\frac{7}{18}''$).

After pulling each section until one of the links broke, the pair remaining was again pulled till one broke, and finally the unbroken remaining link was broken.

The results of the tests were as follows:—

Test No.	Number and Arrangement of Links.		Link which Broke.	Stress at Rupture.	Test No.	Number and Arrangement of Links.		Link which Broke.	Stress at Rupture.
				Pounds.					Pounds.
1	3	Stud, Open, Stud,	S.	87,360	4	1	O.	E. L.	96,000
1	2	O. S.	S.	89,088	4	1	O.	O.	104,000
1	1	O.	E. L.	86,400	5	3	S. O. S.	S.	90,624
1	1	O.	E. L.	74,880	5	1	O.	O.	105,576
2	3	S. O. S.	S.	91,584	6	3	S. O. S.	S.	82,176
2	2	O. O.	O.	99,844	6	2	O. S.	S.	91,776
2	1	O.	E. L.	77,280	6	1	O.	O.	100,128
2	1	O.	O.	82,170	7	3	S. O. S.	S.	79,488
3	3	S. O. S.	S.	96,960	7	2	O. O.	O.	105,600
3	2	O. O.	E. L.	92,544	7	1	O.	E. L.	67,200
3	2	O. O.	O.	104,064	7	1	O.	E. L.	89,280
4	3	S. O. S.	Pin	85,632	7	1	O.	Pin	82,176
4	3	S. O. S.	S.	98,688	7	1	O.	O.	109,632

The bar from which sections Nos. 1 and 2 were made had a tensile strength of 59,000 pounds; Nos. 3 and 4 were from bars with 57,000 pounds; Nos. 5 and 6 from bars with 54,000 pounds; and No. 7 from a bar with 57,700 pounds tensile strength.

In every case in which there were both open and studded links connected, the studded link first broke. In six tests, the open link of $1\frac{1}{8}''$ diameter, of good iron, broke the $1\frac{7}{16}''$ link of inferior iron, and twice the shackle-pin of steel.

The maximum strength of the studded links on the first pull was 96,960 pounds; the minimum, 79,488 pounds; the average of six, 88,030 pounds.

In three cases where a studded link was pulled the second time, the maximum strength was 98,688 pounds; the minimum, 89,088 pounds; and the average, 93,188 pounds.

The maximum strength found in an open link was 109,632 pounds, on a *sixth* pull; the next was 105,576 pounds on a *second* pull; and the minimum, upon any pull, was 82,170 pounds — the average strength of eight being 101,327 pounds; the inferior iron (contract chain-iron), of which the end links were made, breaking upon second and third pulls, at from 67,200 pounds to 96,000 pounds, averaging 82,383 pounds.

From which we deduce, that, of the same iron, an unstudded cable would have exceeded in strength the studded one, in actual strength, over 13,000 pounds, or 15 per cent; and that after having been subjected to stress sufficient to break the studded links, the unstudded cable would have still proved reliable; and, further, that a vessel provided with a studded cable made of this good chain-iron of $1\frac{1}{8}''$ diameter, of which 150 fathoms would weigh five tons, would have possessed more reliable ground-tackle than if the cable had been of the $1\frac{7}{16}''$ contract-iron, weighing eight tons.

During the experiment recorded, several times it happened, that, either through the stress or the recoil, one of the studded links became an open one, by the stud splitting and flying out.

In addition to the evidence given, abstracts from our tests show that in breaking thirty-three sections of links of iron Fx, D, O, and N, which were composed of both studded and unstudded links, in twenty-nine cases the link which broke was a studded one.

From the facts recorded, we feel that we are justified in saying, that beyond doubt, when made of American bar-iron, with cast-iron studs, the studded link is inferior to the unstudded one in strength.

Therefore we place the stud as next to the weld among the elements which tend to prevent the individual links from developing the utmost possible strength.

DESCRIPTION OF METHOD OF TESTING CABLES.

Our records embrace the results of strength, &c., obtained by the rupture of 229 sections of cables, of various diameters and lengths, made from eighteen different irons.

These are given in the tabulated record of breaking strains, arranged in the order of the relative strength.

The history of the test, as cable, of one of the irons (Fx), is given in detail below.

The links were generally arranged as shown in the cuts; the end links, Nos. 1 and 5, and centre link, No. 3, being unstudded, the others studded. The end links were, in some cases, of greater diameter than the links to be tested, in which case they were not recorded in the number of links in section.

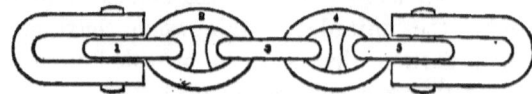

After we had decided upon the superior strength of the unstudded link, our test-sections were prepared with end links of the same size and iron as the other links, but without studs.

The shackle-pins were oval, and made to correspond with the diameter of the links.

Test as Cable of Iron Ex. Links arranged as per Sketch. Elongation recorded when .03″ was observed on No. 2 Link.

Diameter of Iron.	Number of Links.	Stress at First Stretch.	Elongation of			Stress at Rupture.	No. of Link which broke.	Location of Rupture.	Elongation of Unbroken Links.		
			No. 2.	No. 3.	No. 4.				No. 2.	No. 3.	No. 4.
″		Pounds.	″	″	″	Pounds.			″	″	″
1	3	34,800	.03	.11	.03	70,300	4	Q. W.	.50	.62	..
1¼	3	44,400	.03	.16	.03	81,400	2	T. W.	..	.70	.72
1⅜	3	61,100	.03	.14	.05	111,000	2	Q. B.	..	1.00	.70
1½	3	78,000	.05	.24	.03	124,000	3	W.	1.45	..	.75
1⅝	3	80,000	.03	.28	.04	153,000	2	Q. W.	..	1.15	1.00
1¾	3	98,000	.03	.28	.06	168,000	2	Q. W	..	1.85	1.25
1⅞	3	100,000	.03	.26	.04	185,000	2	Q. W.	..	1.20	1.40
1⅞	3	110,000	.03	.22	.03	205,600	3	T. W.	1.60	..	1.30
2	3	117,200	.03	.19	.04	240,000*	..	..	1.50	1.70	1.60

These tests indicate, that with ordinary chain-iron, although the first stretch of the open link is produced by a much lower stress than that which the studded one withstands, yet, upon

* Not broken.

Five ruptures occurred on link No. 2, one on No. 4 studded, and two on open links, in one of which the weld drew. The elongation produced upon the open links by the stress which broke the studded ones was not sufficient to greatly impair their usefulness: the 1″, with original inner diameter of 1.55″, being reduced to 1.40″; the 1¾″, original inner diameter 2.8″, after stress, 2.50″; and the others in proportion, there being sufficient room for the links to traverse freely.

the strain becoming more severe, the disproportion in its effects becomes less, and that frequently the open link is still serviceable after the studded link has broken.

The following abstract shows the extreme variation that we have found in the strength of cable of the same size, made from several irons. We gather from it that a variation of from five to seventeen per cent may be expected in the strength of ordinary cables; and that, if proper care is not exercised in selecting the material, the average variation may rise from twelve to twenty-five per cent of the strength of the strongest.

Variation in Strength of Cables.

Size of Cable.	Number of Irons Represented.	Strength of Cable.		Variation in Strength.		Weak Links omitted of Irons.	Variation in Strength by Including Omitted Links.	
		Maximum.	Minimum.	Pounds.	Per cent of Maximum.		Pounds.	Per cent.
1″	6	79,200	67,600	11,600	14.	P.	18,800	23.7
1⅛	7	89,280	80,900	8,380	9.4	P.	13,200	14.7
1¼	7	122,100	101,700	20,400	16.6	K. M. O.	31,100	25
1 5/16	1	115,000	109,000	6,000	5	M.	40,000	34.7
1⅜	9	137,200	125,000	12,200	8	M. Fx.	42,200	30.7
1 7/16	2	155,040	139,400	15,640	10	. .	. .	. .
1½	9	173,000	147,000	26,000	15	M. K. P.	38,400	22.2
1⅝	12	199,000	168,000	31,000	15.5	M.	74,000	37
1 11/16	2	214,160	194,880	19,280	9	. .	. .	. .
1¾	8	231,300	191,000	40,300	17	Fx.	45,800	19.7
1⅞	2	231,940	204,400	27,540	12	. .	. .	. .
1⅞	6	252,960	215,000	37,960	11	Fx.	47,360	18.6
2	8	283,200	240,000	43,200	15	. .	. .	. .
Average		. .	. .	. .	12.1	. . .	. .	25.1

The excessive variation in case of the 1¾″ is due to the fact that a portion of a lot of excellent chain-iron, C, was composed of very inferior material, which was very irregular in strength; the strongest link in the lot breaking at 231,300 pounds, and five out of eleven sections breaking at less than 200,000 pounds; the minimum being that in the table, 191,000 pounds.

No system of tests made upon cable-bolts alone would have detected with certainty this inferior iron. Had the iron been furnished in thirty-feet bars, each bar would have produced sixteen bolts, with a remainder of twenty-four inches for test purposes, the test of which would have given valuable evidence of the character of the sixteen links.

Weight of Chain-Cables.

The chain-cables manufactured by the ordinary systems are very heavy; and we are led by the results of our investigation to believe that their weight can be reduced advantageously, and as great, if not greater, safety be secured.

The weight and dimensions of various portions of cables of different sizes, and of full cables, of the length ordinarily used, are given in the following table: —

Number and Weight of Links in 150 Fathoms of Cable.

Size.	Number of Links in 150 Fathoms.	Weight of Studs.	Finished Links.			Number of Links in Fathom.	Total Weight of 150 Fathoms Cable.	
			Length.	Width.	Weight.		Studded Link.	Open Link.
		Pounds.			Pounds.		Pounds.	Pounds.
$1''$	2,925	.25	$5\frac{11}{16}''$	$3\frac{9}{16}''$	2.90	$19\frac{1}{2}$	8,665	7,934
$1\frac{1}{16}$	2.775	.25	$6\frac{1}{16}$	$3\frac{11}{16}$	3.43	$18\frac{1}{2}$	9,701	9,008
$1\frac{1}{8}$	2,700	.44	$6\frac{4}{16}$	4	4.22	18	11,650	10,462
$1\frac{3}{16}$	2,550	.44	$6\frac{10}{16}$	$4\frac{2}{16}$	4.89	17	12,726	11,604
$1\frac{1}{4}$	2,450	.50	7	$4\frac{7}{16}$	5.68	16	14,236	13,020
$1\frac{5}{16}$	2,325	.50	$7\frac{5}{16}$	$4\frac{9}{16}$	6.50	$15\frac{1}{2}$	15,442	14,279
$1\frac{3}{8}$	2,250	.62	$7\frac{9}{16}$	$4\frac{15}{16}$	7.52	15	17,326	15,931
$1\frac{7}{16}$	2,100	.62	8	$5\frac{1}{16}$	8.50	14	18,256	16,954
$1\frac{1}{2}$	2,025	.75	$8\frac{4}{16}$	$5\frac{7}{16}$	9.70	$13\frac{1}{2}$	20,143	18,624
$1\frac{9}{16}$	1,950	.75	$8\frac{11}{16}$	$5\frac{9}{16}$	10.87	13	21,697	20,234
$1\frac{5}{8}$	1,875	1.06	9	$5\frac{14}{16}$	12.45	$12\frac{1}{2}$	23,996	22,008
$1\frac{11}{16}$	1,800	1.06	$9\frac{6}{16}$	6	13.81	12	25,510	23,602
$1\frac{3}{4}$	1,725	1.25	$9\frac{12}{16}$	$6\frac{5}{16}$	15.47	$11\frac{1}{2}$	27,480	25,330
$1\frac{13}{16}$	1,650	1.25	$10\frac{3}{16}$	$6\frac{7}{16}$	17.05	11	28.933	26.870
$1\frac{7}{8}$	1,650	1.50	$10\frac{5}{16}$	$6\frac{12}{16}$	19.00	11	32,334	29.859
$1\frac{15}{16}$	1.575	1.50	$10\frac{12}{16}$	$6\frac{14}{16}$	20.80	$10\frac{1}{2}$	33.744	31.382
2	1,500	2.09	$10\frac{14}{16}$	$7\frac{4}{16}$	23 32	10	36,125	32,990
$2\frac{1}{16}$	1,500	2.09	$11\frac{5}{16}$	$7\frac{6}{16}$	25.38	10	39,215	36,080
$2\frac{1}{8}$	1,425	2.25	$11\frac{13}{16}$	$7\frac{10}{16}$	27.72	$9\frac{1}{2}$	40,811	37,605
$2\frac{3}{16}$	1,350	2.25	$12\frac{12}{16}$	$7\frac{12}{16}$	30.04	9	41,864	38,827

Methods by which the Weight of Cables can be reduced in a greater Ratio than the Strength.

Two methods of reducing the weight of chain-cables, without impairing their strength, present themselves as results of our experiments; the first founded upon our investigation of the action of the rolls and our impact tests combined, and the second upon comparative experiments of the strength of studded and open links.

I. We have found, that, when made from the same material, the large bars possess less strength, in proportion to their areas, than the small ones, as opposed to steady strain, and generally much less absolute power to resist sudden strains.

The strength per square inch of a 1⅝″-bar being 54,000 pounds, that of the 2″ would be 50,000 pounds, and the entire strength of the 1⅝″, 112,000 pounds; which is 71 per cent of that of the 2″, viz., 157,000 pounds.

If the two bars, 2″ and 1⅝″, were equally valuable in every respect for cable, and both in link form developed the same percentage of the bar's strength, say 163 per cent, the strength of the 1⅝″ cable would be 182,600 pounds, which is 71 per cent of that of the 2″, viz., 256,000 pounds; while its weight, 23,996 pounds, would be but 66.4 per cent of that of the 2″, viz., 36,125 pounds.

If it be considered that the loss in actual power to resist steady tension is not counterbalanced by the gain in reduced weight, the comparative powers to resist sudden strains should be considered. It is more than probable that the greater work given to the 1⅝″ will have so increased its ductility that its power to resist sudden strains will prove greater than that of the 2″ cable.

These views are borne out by many of our experiments, from which we will select the bars of iron N for comparison. This iron was sent to us by a prominent manufacturer, in answer to an order for "samples of best cable-iron."

The 2″-bar had tenacity 51,748 pounds, and, when broken by

tension, had a very slight reduction of area and elongation: broken by impact, it proved very brittle, and, while in no ways nicked or injured, would break like a pipe-stem by moderate blows.

Tested as cable, the links developed but 141 per cent of the bar's strength; viz., 232,000 pounds.

The $1\frac{3}{8}''$-bar, with tenacity 56,344 pounds, when tested by tension, reduced in area to 60 per cent of the original, and elongated 23 per cent.

Tested by impact, it proved fairly tough, deflecting to over 60° before breaking, and, when circled with a score, resisted to a greater extent than did the $2''$ in its normal condition.

Tested as cable, the links developed 164 per cent of the bar's strength, breaking at 195,500 pounds, or at 84 per cent of the strength of the $2''$.

In this case, there can be no doubt but that the smaller and lighter cable would have proved the most reliable.

Irregularity in strength is a great fault in cable-iron: this is more apt to occur in large than in small bars; one reason for which is, that irregularity in heating the piles produces irregularity in strength, and to this the large bars are more greatly exposed than the small ones. The pile and resultant bar of $2''$ weighs four or five hundred pounds, and, while passing through the roll, is, of course, much more difficult to handle than a lighter pile or bar: there are greater liabilities of "buckling" and "bending;" and, while the workmen are mauling the bar to straighten it, the next bar to be rolled is being delayed in the furnace, and the effects of variation in the heat are not provided against by regulating the latter. It seems but natural, that, if the pile for a small bar is heated enough for rolling in one hour, portions of the large pile are, in the same time, equally ready, and that by longer delay in the furnace they become overheated.

The effect of overheating is to lower both the elastic limit and the strength.

Irregularity in the workmanship by which the links are

manufactured produces irregular strength in the cable. To this the larger bars are exposed to a greater extent than the smaller ones: the *weld* is less apt to be perfect. A small bar is, when at the right heat, welded by a few quick blows; and the time of the operation is not great enough to allow the iron to become cool. With a large bar it is different. It requires more and harder blows, and more time; and, if at the right heat when the operation is begun, it may be too cool before it is ended, or, in order that it shall not be, it may be heated a little too much on the start; the surface of the weld is greater, and is more exposed to the danger of interposition of ashes, dust, or scoria, either of which will prevent a perfect weld.

Finally, if the cable be finished without any accidental defect, the proof of the 2″ so far exceeds that of the 1⅝″, in proportion to its strength, that it is possible that the strength it may have had will be lowered by it.

For the reasons assigned, we are of the opinion that the margin of safety secured by the use of a cable of 1⅝″ iron, weighing twelve tons, is equally great as by the use of the 2″, weighing eighteen tons.

II. The second method of reducing the weight of cables consists in the substitution of open for studded links.

There exists a strong prejudice against the use of cables made from links without studs. This prejudice is based upon the opinion which is very generally entertained, that, first, the open link is not as strong as the studded one; second, that, owing to the want of the support given to the sides by the stud when used, the open link will collapse at a much lower strain than the studded one will, and that this collapse will be so great that the links will nip each other, and become rigid; and, third, that the liability of the relative position of the links to become misplaced is greater with the open than with the studded links, from which cause jams may occur in the hawse-pipe when the cable is running out, or, after having remained some time with a slack cable, a sudden squall, tautening it, might produce the same effect.

THE CABLE.

The first of these objections, viz., that the open link is weaker than the studded one, our experiments show to be without foundation. The contrary is the case under all circumstances.

We are led, by the results of our tests, to doubt that the second objection exists to the extent generally supposed. We find, that, in all cases, the open links *begin* to change form at a lower stress than the studded ones; but the sides having straightened somewhat, the stress is soon resisted by the tenacity of the material itself, and unless the iron is very soft and ductile (much more so than is usually the case with chain-iron), the closure does not continue to be rapid; and at an extreme stress, sufficient to rupture the studded link, if there be one in the section under test, the closure has not been so great as to unfit the open links for service.

With irons F and O, both extremely ductile, some of the open links were too much closed for service, but others were not, after having resisted the stress which broke the studded links. Such iron, however, will not often be made into cables; and we have, to a certain extent, a resource by which this early closure of the sides may be delayed with all irons.

A cable made of bolts of $\frac{1}{8}$ of an inch greater diameter, without studs, will possess fully twenty per cent more strength than the smaller studded cable, and will weigh but a trifle more. For instance, the total weight of 150 fathoms or ten sections of $1\frac{1}{2}''$ studded cable would be 20,143 pounds; and that of 150 fathoms or ten sections of $1\frac{5}{8}''$ open cable would be 22,008 pounds.

Thus the difference in weight would be but 1,865 pounds.

The probable strength of the $1\frac{1}{2}''$ studded cable would be, at greatest, 157,000 pounds; that of the $1\frac{5}{8}''$, if studded, 182,000 pounds, and if unstudded considerably more; the minimum difference of 25,000 pounds being nearly sixteen per cent of the entire strength of the $1\frac{1}{2}''$ cable. And, as the action of the studs tends to pry open such welds as may not be perfect, the chances for regularity in strength are much increased by its omission. And it is more than probable that the extreme stress at which the 1¼" would break would not close the links of 1⅝" to such extent as to render them unserviceable.

The third objection to the use of open-link cables is that it is presumed that they are more liable to become fouled and kinked than the studded-link cable, while being stowed in the chain-locker, or when slack, and the vessel changes her position without tautening the cable.

There are reasons based upon facts which actually exist, connected with the process of manufacture, which justify us in the assumption that the danger from this cause is not so great with open-link as with studded-link cables. [These reasons are given at length in the original report.]

COMPARISON OF RESULTS OBTAINED BY TENSION UPON SECTIONS OF CABLE-LINKS, AND UPON BARS OF THE IRON FROM WHICH LINKS WERE MADE.

It was considered that if there existed, as seemed probable, a relationship between the strength and other properties of the round bar, and those of the links made from it, it would be a valuable result to determine such relationship, and to find to how great an extent it could be depended upon, and within what margins it existed; inasmuch as the simple and inexpensive test of tension upon a portion of a bar would provide data by which the probable strength of a cable made from it could be judged.

The following tables have been prepared for the purpose of developing this relationship, and finding its margins.

We find that with iron of moderate tenacity, and with good welding properties, the percentage of the bar's strength, which is carried with great uniformity into the link, is from 160 to 175 per cent; that, with irons of unsuitable qualities, this percentage is frequently low and frequently high, it being very irregular, and averages of less than 155 per cent, made up of very irregular factors, are common; and that with the best chain-iron, although there may be links which develop over 175 per cent, such cases are rare.

Comparison of Strength of Cable-Links and Round Bars.

Iron A.

Cable Links.							Round Bars.					Ratios of Links & Bars.	
Diameter of Bar.	No. of Tests averaged.	Stress in Pounds. First Stretch was observed.	Stress in Pounds. Fracture took Place.	Stress in Pounds. Borne by end per square inch sectional Area.	Ratio between first Stretch and Fracture.	Stretch of Unbroken Links.	Number of Bars in Test.	Stress in Pounds. First Stretch was observed.	Stress in Pounds. Fracture took Place.	Stress in Pounds. Per square inch Original Area.	Ratio between Stresses of first Stretch and Fracture.	Ratio between Bars and Links.	Ratio between Links and Bars.
1"	3	28,160	71,328	88,441	39.5	1.15"	3	28,127	44,126	54,690	63.9	61.9	161.3
1⅛	2	37,920	89,040	88,773	42.5	1.15	3	27,488	53,997	53,900	51.2	60.6	164.9
1¼	2	47,040	114,680	92,689	41.	1.2	3	33,888	66,112	53,879	51.3	57.7	173.5
1⅜	2	58,080	134,400	91,180	43.2	1.5	3	49,600	78,944	53,557	62.8	58.7	170.3
1½	2	68,650	153,600	86,926	44.7	1.65	2	50,880	91,680	51,884	55.4	59.7	167.5
1⅝	2	76,320	174,260	84,551	43.7	1.35	2	66,240	111,984	54,334	59.1	64.3	155.6
1¾	2	86,400	214,560	89,213	40.3	1.85	2	70,840	123,840	51,509	57.2	57.6	173.
1⅞	1	96,000	252,960	91,125	38.	2.	2	79,650	141,120	50,854	56.	56.7	176.
2	11	......	264,002	84,023	....	1.56	9	91,038	157,588	50,171	57.8	59.	168.9
						Iron B.							
1 7/16	13	61,721	149,790	92,293	41.1	1.32	4	52,607	84,862	52,287	61.8	56.7	176.4
1 11/16	4	87,937	198,144	86,637	44.4	1.23	3	74,113	118,273	52,895	62.7	59.9	166.7
1 13/16	4	94,143	221,650	85,910	41.5	....	3	87,743	137,023	53,109	63.	62.1	161.7
						Iron C.							
*1⅛	1	48,600	101,800	102,414	47.6	....	2	31,710	57,125	57,470	55.5	56.1	178.2
*1¼	2	61,450	123,450	98,573	49.8	....	1	39,840	71,040	57,897	56.	57.5	173.6
*1⅜	2	75,850	133,400	89,831	56.8	....	1	46,080	81,600	54,949	56.4	61.1	163.4
*1 7/16	1	......	149,600	92,175	....	....	1	53,000	84,000	51,756	63.1	56.1	178.
1½	7	65,700	157,900	89,360	44.4	....	5	61,440	97,921	55,404	62.5	61.2	161.9
1⅝	7	82,229	180,500	87,030	45.5	....	4	68,880	115,749	55,879	59.4	64.4	155.5
1¾	13	90,554	199,830	83,009	45.5	....	5	75,420	130,835	54,410	57.1	65.9	153.
						Iron D. First Lot.							
*1⅛	2	37,200	96,200	96,780	38.6	....	2	29,300	54,360	54,687	53.9	56.6	176.3
*1¼	2	53,800	123,800	100,896	43.1	....	1	34,560	68,160	55,550	50.7	55.	181.
*1⅜	2	57,600	143,400	96,565	39.8	....	1	47,040	81,600	54,949	57.6	56.8	175.7
*1½	2	71,800	178,300	100,905	40.3	....	1	48,960	92,160	52,155	53.1	51.6	193.4
*1⅝	1	85,000	199,700	96,287	42.5	....	1	62,400	111,360	53,695	56.	55.7	179.2
*1¾	1	94,100	231,400	96,216	41.	....	1	66,900	126,720	52,699	52.8	54.7	182.6
*1⅞	1	94,600	238,100	86,236	40.	....	1	76,800	142,080	51,459	54.	59.6	167.6
*2	1	134,400	276,500	88,000	48.5	....	1	89,760	160,700	51,146	55.8	58.1	172.
						Iron D. Second Lot.							
1	1	36,200	79,200	100,843	45.7	1.25	1	26,300	48,000	61,115	54.8	60.6	165.
1⅛	1	45,000	87,500	88,814	51.4	1.55	1	33,100	58,700	59,582	56.4	67.	149.
1¼	1	55,200	113,000	90,617	48.8	1.60	1	39,900	72,300	57,979	55.2	64.	156.3
1⅜	1	71,500	137,200	91,711	52.1	2.25	1	47,500	86,800	58,021	54.7	63.2	158.
1½	1	80,100	173,000	97,906	46.3	2.50	1	58,200	101,200	56,505	57.5	58.5	170.8
1⅝	1	90,000	182,000	88,306	49.5	3.	1	63,200	110,500	53,614	57.2	60.7	164.8
1¾	1	99,000	204,000	84,823	48.5	3.10	1	76,700	128,600	53,472	59.6	63.	158.6
1⅞	1	112,300	215,000	76,468	52.2	3.75	1	90,000	149,000	53,100	60.5	69.3	144.2
2	1	116,000	240,000	77,947	Not	br'k'n	2	105,400	145,950	47,648	72.3	60.8	164.4

* The tests marked * were upon single links, the others upon sections of cable.

WROUGHT-IRON AND CHAIN-CABLES.

Iron E.

Diameter of Bar.	No. of Tests averaged.	Cable Links. Stress in Pounds.			Ratio between first Stretch and Fracture.	Stretch of Unbroken Links.	Number of Bars in Test.	Round Bars. Stress in Pounds.			Ratio between Stresses of first Stretch and Fracture.	Ratios of Links & Bars.	
		First Stretch was observed.	Fracture took place.	Borne by end per square inch sectional Area.				First Stretch was observed.	Fracture took place.	Per square inch Original Area.		Ratio between Bars and Links.	Ratio between Links and Bars.
*1¼	4	43,700	87,650	84,360	49.9	....	1	34,848	55,152	53,097	63.1	62.9	158.0
*1¼	4	44,625	113,650	91,138	39.3	....	1	26,320	67,200	53,893	42.1	59.2	169.1
*1¼	4	54,500	134,900	88,925	40.4	....	1	39,360	79,296	52,254	49.6	58.8	170.2
*1¼	2	68,650	160,650	90,916	42.7	....	1	50,060	97,920	55,415	59.3	61.	164.
*1¼	2	72,250	189,800	90,991	38.1	....	1	57,792	108,384	51,940	53.3	57.1	175.1
*1¼	1	91,000	221,500	92,099	41.	....	1	63,840	124,128	51,606	51.4	56.	178.4
*1¼	2	93,800	233,600	82,858	40.2	....	2	76,608	142,991	50,580	53.5	61.3	163.2

Iron F. First Lot.

1	1	28,500	86,400	87,698	33.	.60	3	32,993	53,053	53,850	62.1	61.4	162.8
1	1	50,000	101,700	82,855	49.1	....	2	39,360	64,990	52,970	60.5	63.9	156.4
1	1	51,000	119,000	79,545	42.9	.90	2	48,190	77,235	51,296	62.3	64.9	154.
1	1	60,540	155,500	88,002	38.9	1.00	2	56,640	91,875	51,994	61.6	59.	169.2
1⅛	1	71,000	174,700	84,764	40.6	1.00	2	69,890	107,520	52,163	64.9	61.5	162.5
1⅛	1	76,400	203,500	84,615	37.5	1.90	2	77,520	121,920	50,690	63.5	59.9	166.9
1⅛	1	83,500	230,900	83,177	36.1	2.4	2	91,295	140,925	51,039	64.7	60.6	163.8
2	1	105,000	268,750	86,414	39.1	....	2	85,950	152,260	48,956	56.4	56.6	176.5

Iron F. Third Lot.

1	1	35,600	67,600	84,372	52.6	....	2	31,300	41,600	51,921	75.2	61.5	162.4
1⅛	1	47,600	85,000	84,745	56.	....	2	35,600	50,300	50,149	70.7	59.1	168.8
1	1	55,000	107,600	87,693	51.1	....	2	48,600	64,700	52,729	75.1	60.1	166.
1	1	65,600	128,600	85,962	51.	....	2	58,500	78,300	52,339	74.7	60.8	164.2
1	1	70,600	150,500	85,172	47.	....	2	62,000	89,800	50,820	69.	59.6	167.6
1	1	......	......	......	....	....	2	72,000	103,500	50,529	69.5	....	....
1	1	90,000	197,600	83,095	45.5	....	2	85,500	120,200	50,547	71.2	60.8	164.6
1⅛	1	90,000	215,600	78,514	41.7	....	2	97,800	136,600	49,744	71.7	63.3	157.8
2	1	100,600	233,600	73,621	43.	....	2	113,800	151,900	47,872	74.8	65.	148.8
1	3	1,533	3,775	76,003	40.7	....	1	......	2,919	59,585	....	77.6	129.3
1	4	3,875	8,916	80,647	43.7	....	4	4,410	5,949	54,090	74.1	67.1	149.9
1	3	6,600	16,933	86,100	39.1	....	1	7,680	10,343	52,772	74.3	61.2	163.7
1	2	5,800	25,400	85,519	20.9	....	3	10,834	15,924	52,051	67.9	62.7	159.5
1	2	10,000	34,700	74,460	29.	....	3	16,748	23,024	50,764	72.8	66.9	150.6
1	2	15,805	46,400	74,999	....	....	3	21,097	31,317	50,716	67.4	67.7	148.1

Iron Fx. First Lot.

1	1	34,800	70,300	86,036	49.5	1.12	5	27,680	45,040	55,770	61.5	64.	156.8
1⅛	1	44,400	81,400	79,725	54.5	1.42	5	35,500	57,620	56,434	61.5	70.8	141.2
1⅛	1	64,100	111,000	90,464	55.	1.70	5	43,100	68,460	55,253	63.	61.7	162.
1⅛	1	78,000	124,000	82,887	62.9	2.25	5	50,480	80,360	52,968	64.8	62.8	154.2
1⅛	1	80,000	153,000	88,593	52.3	2.15	5	60,620	94,520	53,491	64.1	61.8	161.8
1⅛	1	98,000	168,000	81,513	58.3	3.11	5	70,560	110,140	53,537	64.	65.6	152.4
1⅛	1	100,000	185,000	76,923	54.	2.60	5	87,960	129,500	53,846	67.9	70.	142.8
1⅛	1	110,800	205,600	74,063	53.9	2.90	5	98,920	146,780	52,875	67.3	71.4	140.
2	1	117,200	240,000	76,384	Not br'k'n	4.8	5	108,980	163,420	52,011	66.6	....	....

* The tests marked * were upon single links, the others upon sections of cable.

THE CABLE.

Iron Fx. Third Lot.

Diameter of Bar.	No. of Tests averaged.	Cable Links. Stress in Pounds. First Stretch was observed.	Cable Links. Stress in Pounds. Fracture took place.	Cable Links. Stress in Pounds. Borne by end per square inch sectional at Area.	Ratio between first Stretch and Fracture.	Stretch of Unbroken Links.	Number of Bars in Test.	Round Bars. Stress in Pounds. First Stretch was observed.	Round Bars. Stress in Pounds. Fracture took place.	Round Bars. Per square inch Original Area.	Ratio between Stresses of first Stretch and Fracture.	Ratios of Links & Bars. Ratio between Bars and Links.	Ratios of Links & Bars. Ratio between Links and Bars.
1	1	34,500	69,600	88,617	49.6	....	2	28,500	42,350	53,915	67.3	60.8	164.4
1⅛	1	39,600	86,000	85,724	46.	....	2	34,800	54,300	54,644	63.5	63.7	157.
1¼	1	49,000	105,000	84,202	46.7	....	2	41,800	66,400	53,247	62.9	63.2	158.
1⅜	1	60,000	126,800	83,586	47.3	....	2	52,500	80,000	52,733	65.6	63.	158.6
1½	1	70,600	152,800	85,315	46.2	....	2	62,400	94,600	52,819	65.9	61.9	161.6
1⅝	1	83,000	179,000	85,789	46.4	....	2	70,000	111,300	53,329	62.9	63.1	160.8
1¾	1	100,000	190,600	80,237	52.5	....	2	81,000	126,100	53,154	64.8	66.2	151.2
1⅞	1	109,000	229,000	83,394	47.6	....	2	96,200	146,500	53,361	65.7	64.	156.4
2	1	118,000	236,600	75,938	49.5	....	2	104,500	159,500	50,763	65.5	66.8	149.6

Iron G.

*1	1	......	160,100	90,605	....	....	1	62,600	91,800	51,958	68.1	57.3	174.4
*1⅛	1	......	195,200	94,118	....	....	1	69,100	106,200	51,205	65.6	54.4	183.2
*1¼	1	......	215,200	89,480	....	....	1	87,200	121,200	50,395	71.9	56.3	177.6

Iron H.

*1	1	......	170,000	96,208	....	....	1	53,000	92,700	52,462	57.1	54.5	183.4
*1⅛	1	......	204,100	97,409	....	....	1	60,900	108,500	52,314	56.1	53.2	188.
*1¼	1	......	225,200	93,638	....	....	1	67,000	129,400	53,800	51.7	57.5	174.

Iron J.

*1	1	......	157,600	89,190	....	....	1	......	90,200	51,047	....	57.2	174.6
*1⅛	1	......	120,000	57,859	....	....	1	......	109,400	52,748	....	91.2	109.6
*1¼	1	......	222,700	92,600	....	....	1	......	128,100	53,264	....	57.5	173.8

Iron K.

1⅛	1	39,400	84,500	85,001	46.6	1.70	3	37,120	60,096	60,458	61.7	71.1	140.6
1⅛	1	47,000	96,000	78,240	49.	.50	2	44,640	72,960	59,461	61.1	76.	131.4
1¼	1	58,000	125,800	84,714	42.2	.47	2	46,080	82,848	55,790	55.6	65.8	150.6
1⅜	1	57,600	143,000	80,925	31.2	.87	2	59,040	101,280	57,317	58.2	70.8	141.2
1½	2	72,900	177,450	85,559	41.	.86	4	72,640	118,463	57,132	63.1	66.8	149.7
1⅝	1	72,500	172,800	71,850	42.	.65	1	79,680	139,200	57,874	57.2	80.5	124.1
1¾	1	97,000	246,800	89,387	39.	1.00	2	85,680	154,080	55,803	55.6	62.4	160.
2	1	104,000	258,900	82,400	40.	1.00	2	101,280	191,520	58,890	52.8	74.	135.2

Iron L.

*1	1	......	193,200	109,337	....	....	1	50,500	123,300	69,779	41.	63.8	156.6
*1⅛	1	......	163,600	78,881	....	....	1	92,200	139,200	67,116	66.2	85.	116.2
*1¼	1	......	254,600	105,862	....	....	1	87,200	145,000	60,291	60.	56.9	175.6

Iron M.

1	6	53,700	117,716	98,905	45.7	....	20	......	65,960	53,752	....	57.3	178.4
1⅛	22	59,390	116,628	83,341	51.4	....	115	54,789	83,300	55,991	65.8	72.0	140.5
1¼	6	71,700	152,467	86,270	47.2	....	162	61,808	97,250	54,480	62.9	63.8	159.3
1⅜	2	{80,000 / 79,000}	{125,000 / 180,000}	{60,270 / 86,788}	{64. / 43.7}	....	10	74,510	119,750	57,402	61.7	....	....

* The tests marked * were upon single links, the others upon sections of cable.

WROUGHT-IRON AND CHAIN-CABLES.

Iron M. Second Lot.

Diameter of Bar.	No. of Tests averaged.	CABLE LINKS.					ROUND BARS.					RATIOS OF LINKS & BARS.	
		Stress in Pounds.			Ratio between first Stretch and Fracture.	Stretch of Unbroken Links.	Number of Bars in Test.	Stress in Pounds.			Ratio between Stresses of first Stretch and Fracture.	Ratio between Bars and Links.	Ratio between Links and Bars.
		First Stretch was observed.	Fracture took place.	Borne by end per square inch sectional at Area.				First Stretch was observed.	Fracture took place.	Per square inch Original Area.			
1¼	5	......	{ 92,000 to 114,000 }	{ 75,244 to 92,909 }	....	....	53	......	72,700	59,248	....	{ 63.8 to 79.0 }	{ 126.5 to 156.8 }
1 5⁄16	4	......	{ 77,000 to 117,000 }	{ 57,650 to 86,474 }	....	....	20	......	76,800	56,761	....	{ 65.6 to 99.7 }	{ 100.3 to 152.3 }
1⅜	3	......	{ 113,100 to 133,000 }	{ 76,094 to 89,562 }	....	....	18	......	84,300	56,777	....	{ 63.4 to 74.6 }	{ 134. to 157.7 }
1½	5	......	{ 155,000 to 169,000 }	{ 88,058 to 95,642 }	....	....	47	......	99,429	56,270	....	{ 58.8 to 63.9 }	{ 156.4 to 169.9 }
1⅝	1	......	187,000	90,175	....	....	5	......	113,760	54,851	....	60.8	164.4
1 11⁄16	1	......	207,000	92,576	....	....	5	......	127,700	57,115	....	61.7	162.1
1¾	5	......	{ 212,000 to 225,600 }	{ 88,149 to 93,804 }	....	....	29	......	137,092	57,003	....	{ 60.8 to 64.7 }	{ 154.7 to 164.5 }
1 13⁄16	4	......	{ 210,000 to 228,000 }	{ 81,395 to 88,605 }	....	....	24	......	142,367	55,181	....	{ 61.4 to 67.8 }	{ 147.6 to 167.6 }
2	3	......	{ 255,000 to 276,000 }	{ 81,158 to 91,661 }	....	....	47	......	171,490	54,580	....	{ 61.7 to 67.3 }	{ 148.6 to 162.1 }

Iron N.

1¼	1	45,000	85,000	84,915	53.	1.76	2	32,300	56,200	56,143	57.5	66.1	151.2
1¼	1	58,000	105,000	85,574	53.8	2.06	2	40,800	60,300	56,478	58.1	66.	151.4
1¼	1	70,100	126,400	84,492	55.4	2.52	2	50,300	81,200	54,277	62.	64.2	155.4
1¼	1	80,000	152,200	87,270	52.5	2.77	2	60,500	93,400	53,555	64.7	61.4	162.8
1¼	1	96,200	195,500	92,566	49.2	3.60	2	75,800	119,000	56,344	63.6	60.9	164.2
1¼	1	110,300	201,100	85,538	54.8	1.75	2	80,600	129,350	55,018	62.3	64.3	161.8
1¼	1	116,200	223,700	81,463	51.9	3.40	2	92,300	140,150	51,037	66.1	62.6	159.6
2	1	118,000	232,000	73,116	50.8	2.60	2	103,000	164,200	51,748	62.6	70.8	141.2

Iron O.

1	1	31,400	68,000	84,872	46.2	....	1	30,000	46,000	57,363	65.2	67.6	148.
1⅛	1	35,000	80,900	85,131	43.3	....	1	30,800	50,400	53,035	61.1	62.3	160.6
1¼	1	45,800	95,500	77,832	48.	....	1	36,900	61,400	50,040	60.1	64.3	155.6
1⅜	1	51,200	125,400	87,631	41.8	....	1	50,000	72,400	50,919	69.	57.7	173.2
1½	1	60,000	155,500	86,823	38.6	....	1	58,000	91,400	50,919	63.4	58.8	170.
1⅝	1	74,500	180,000	87,336	41.4	....	1	70,100	108,000	52,401	64.9	60.	166.6
1¾	1	90,000	207,000	89,070	43.5	....	1	75,000	116,500	50,129	64.3	56.3	177.6
1⅞	1	102,000	237,000	87,288	43.	....	1	83,800	129,000	47,478	65.	54.4	183.8
2	1	119,800	238,000	75,747	50.3	....	1	98,700	151,600	48,249	65.1	63.7	156.

Iron P.

Cable Links.							Round Bars.					Ratios of Links & Bars.	
Diameter of Bar.	No. of Tests averaged.	Stress in Pounds. First Stretch was observed.	Stress in Pounds. Fracture took place.	Stress in Pounds. Borne by end per square inch sectional at Area.	Ratio between first Stretch and Fracture.	Stretch of Unbroken Links.	Number of Bars in Test.	Stress in Pounds. First Stretch was observed.	Stress in Pounds. Fracture took place.	Stress in Pounds. Per square inch Original Area.	Ratio between Stresses of first Stretch and Fracture.	Ratio between Bars and Links.	Ratio between Links and Bars.
1¼	2	......	112,320	88,612	....	....	2	45,124	70,704	55,782	61.4	....	....
1 5/16	6	52,800	110,000	91,317	47.6	....	94	48,550	74,427	54,518	65.3	....	....
1⅜	1	......	134,592	89,968	....	....	1	46,080	78,624	52,556	58.6	58.4	....
1 7/16	6	61,800	141,000	86,876	43.8	....	2	......	89,300	53,345	....	....	157.9
1½	1	......	134,592	74,196	....	....	1	53,760	95,904	52,808	56.1	71.2	....
2	1	125,000	256,320	80,000	48.8	....	1	96,000	159,840	49,872	63.	62.4	160.4

Iron P. Second Lot.

1	1	38,000	60,400	78,461	62.9	....	2	30,200	44,500	57,807	67.9	73.7	135.8
1⅛	1	45,200	76,000	77,141	59.5	....	2	40,700	56,500	57,280	72.	....	....
1¼	1	50,400	122,100	94,871	43.1	....	2	47,450	73,200	56,876	64.8	60.	166.8
1⅜	1	60,000	118,400	76,933	50.7	....	2	53,500	85,000	55,230	62.9	71.6	139.6
1½	1	73,600	156,000	85,950	47.2	....	2	60,650	98,300	54,159	61.7	63.	158.6
1⅝	1	86,000	199,000	94,270	43.2	....	2	70,800	117,500	55,634	60.2	75.3	169.4
1¾	1	106,000	212,000	86,143	50.	....	2	82,400	130,050	52,844	63.4	61.3	163.
1⅞	1	115,000	233,000	83,933	49.4	....	2	89,700	145,200	52,305	61.8	62.3	160.4
2	1	129,000	242,000	Not bro	ken	....	2	101,150	161,300	50,834	62.7	....	....

Iron Px.

1¼	1	53,000	116,000	93,023	45.7	....	2	42,300	70,250	56,334	59.5	60.6	165.2
1⅜	1	71,400	156,000	87,102	45.8	....	2	62,000	97,350	54,354	64.	62.4	160.2
1½	1	84,600	196,200	91,003	43.1	....	2	70,600	115,500	54,689	61.1	58.8	160.9
1⅝	1	98,000	209,800	86,231	46.7	....	2	82,500	131,000	54,212	62.5	63.1	158.4
1¾	1	108,200	236,000	85,943	45.8	....	2	88,600	142,000	51,762	62.2	60.	166.2
2	1	120,000	242,000	Not bro	ken	....	1	98,600	168,800	53,198	58.4	....	....

SECTION VI.

PROOF STRAINS FOR CHAIN-CABLES.

EFFECTS PRODUCED BY THE USE OF THE STRAINS PRE-
SCRIBED BY THE ADMIRALTY PROOF TABLE. — DISCUSSION
OF THE PRINCIPLES UPON WHICH "PROOF STRAINS"
SHOULD BE BASED. — PROOF TABLE CALCULATED UPON
SUCH PRINCIPLES.

A FINISHED cable has yet a final ordeal to undergo before it is issued for service, — one which may prove disastrous to its value, even if it has escaped every danger that has accompanied its manufacture. It is to be "proved;" which means that each of the fifteen-fathom "sections" of which it is composed is to be subjected to a tensional strain sufficient to make it probable that the presence of any defective links will be made manifest, that they may be removed, and replaced by others.

As tension in excess will probably injure the cable, it becomes a matter of importance to fix upon a strain for each size, which, while sufficient to insure the detection of unduly weak links, *will not produce them.* Most American manufacturers of cable use for each size a stress which is prescribed by the standard proof table of the British Admiralty; and their cables are sold with a guaranty that they have been so proved.

Our experiments lead us to doubt the wisdom of thus applying this English standard to measure American material. We consider, that, as applied to cables made of American bar-iron, this standard is faulty in two important respects: —

First, The stress prescribed by it for every size of cable is too great.

Second, The stresses for the different sizes are unequal in their proportion to the strength of the links.

And we assign the following reasons for these opinions: —

First, The stress for all sizes is based upon the assumption that the cable bolts of all diameters possess a strength equal to sixty thousand pounds per square inch. Few bars of American iron have this strength, and, when they have, their cost precludes their use as cable-iron; and, as has been shown in the investigations by tension, although this strength may be found in the small bars, it is not found in the large sizes of the same iron.

Secondly, If the bars of all sizes did possess this strength, the "proof" is still too great; for it probably exceeds by a considerable amount the *elastic limit* of the links.

The table as furnished to the committee by two prominent manufacturers, viz., Messrs. J. B. Carr & Co. of Troy, and Mr. H. L. Fearing of Boston, is herewith given, that the discussion which follows may be clearly understood.

Size.	Column 1. Stress in		Column 2. Stress in		Column 3. Stress in	
	Tons.	Pounds.	Tons.	Pounds.	Tons.	Pounds.
1"	18	40,320	18	40,320	18	40,320
$1\frac{1}{16}$	20	44,800	20	44,800	20.32	45,517
$1\frac{1}{8}$	23	51,520	23	51,520	22.78	51,030
$1\frac{3}{16}$	26	58,200	25	55,960	25.38	56,857
$1\frac{1}{4}$	28	62,720	29	64.960	28.12	63,000
$1\frac{5}{16}$	30	67,200	31	69,440	31.01	69,457
$1\frac{3}{8}$	34	76,160	34	76,160	34.03	76,230
$1\frac{7}{16}$	37	82,880	37	82,880	37.22	83,317
$1\frac{1}{2}$	41	91,800	41	91,800	40.50	90,720
$1\frac{9}{16}$	44	98,500	43	96,320	43.04	98,437
$1\frac{5}{8}$	48	107,520	48	107,520	47.53	106,470
$1\frac{11}{16}$	52	116,480	51	114,240	51.25	114,817
$1\frac{3}{4}$	56	125,440	56	125,440	55.12	123,480
$1\frac{13}{16}$	60	134,400	59	132,160	59.05	132,275
$1\frac{7}{8}$	64	143,360	64	143,360	63.38	141,750
$1\frac{15}{16}$	68	152,320	68	152,320	67.57	151,357
2	72	161,280	72	161,280	72	161,280
$2\frac{1}{16}$	..	....	76	171,360	76.59	171,517
$2\frac{1}{8}$	80	179,200	81.3	181,120	81.28	182,070
$2\frac{3}{16}$	..	....	..	....	86.13	192,937
$2\frac{1}{4}$	88	197,120	91.1	204,064	91.11	204,120

The formula upon which column 3 is calculated is one embodied as a rule as follows:—

"For proof of each size, square the number of eighths of an inch in the diameter of the bar, and multiply the result by 630," the result being the stress in pounds. Thus: 1″, 8 eighths, squared = 64, and 64 × 630 = 40,320 pounds."

Our experiments show that the elastic limit of the large bars is generally lower than that of the small ones of the same iron. Hence the irregular effect of the proof strains becomes a dangerous one.

The practical and actual results which we have found to occur through the use of this table, and which have doubtless occurred with many cables proved by it, but which have *not* been *found*, are that the stress is so great that it always exceeds the elastic limit of the links, and frequently cracks them.

A few such results will be given. Six sections, each five fathoms in length, were made up from good chain-iron; three were of 1½″, and three of 1⅝″: all were "proved" by the Admiralty Table, and after proof inspected in the shop; all were "passed" as sound; but upon examination by aid of a magnifying-glass fourteen of the 387 links were found to be cracked.

In the following table the strength of the strongest and weakest links made from several of the best of the chain-irons we have examined is given, with the ratio borne to such strength by the Admiralty proof strains for the sizes:—

Iron.	Strength of Large Links.			Admiralty Proof, percentage of		Strength of Small Links.			Admiralty Proof, percentage of	
	Size.	Strongest.	Weakest.	Strongest.	Weakest.	Size.	Strongest.	Weakest.	Strongest.	Weakest.
		Pounds.	Pounds.				Pounds.	Pounds.		
A......	2″	283,000	248,000	57	65	1″	72,670	69,600	55.5	58
C......	1¾	231,300	191,000	53	64	1⅛	96,960	74,488	52.5	65
D......	1⅞	215,000	......	66	....	1	79,200	......	51.3	....
F......	1⅞	215,600	......	66	....	1	67,600	......	59.6	....
N......	1⅞	225,700	......	63.3	....	1⅛	85,600	......	60	....
O......	1⅞	237,000	......	60	....	1	68,000	......	59.3	....
P......	1⅞	233,000	......	60.8	....	1¼	122,100	......	51.2	....
Average..	....	......	......	61.	64.5	....	....	......	55.6	61.6

Convinced by the evidence which has been given, that proving American cables by this standard was a fruitful source of weakened cables, we were also aware, that, in recommending that it should be no longer used, we should, if the advice were followed, deprive manufacturers of good cables of a safeguard against competition by those who might unchecked use inferior iron. We have therefore considered it essential that we should provide a substitute which would, in our judgment, prescribe strains which would fully *prove* cables, and not be liable to *injure* them. We submit such a table, which is based upon the two principles, that a proof strain should not greatly exceed the elastic limit, and that the strength of a cable is equal only to that of its weakest link. In the preparation of this table it was first necessary for us to establish within reasonable limits the probable maximum and minimum strength of cables of various sizes, and the elastic limit of the links. Neither of these factors can be fixed definitely: there are many causes which tend to produce great differences, both in the strength and elastic limit of links made from the same bar. The most important of these causes is the liability of the welds, which at the best are the weak spots of all links, to lack uniformity; and no rules can be given which will insure uniform work from a number of chain-welders. We were therefore compelled to base our table upon data which, at the best, could be considered as but indicating probabilities.

Assuming as a standard of perfection the characteristics of a bar, which when made into a link should develop twice the original strength of the bar, we considered that the iron which approached most closely and with uniformity this standard was that which should be considered as the most suitable for cables. We have the records of the strains at which a large number of bars in their normal condition were ruptured by tension, and of many sections of cable made from them, which are incorporated in the "Tables of Comparative Action of Bars and Links." From these tables we have made the following abstracts which enable us to arrive at conclusions as to the probable strength of cables made from irons varying in characteristics:—

WROUGHT-IRON AND CHAIN-CABLES.

Ratio of Strength of Sections of Links to that of the Bars from which they were made.

[DETAIL BY SIZES.]

Size in Inches.	A.	B.	C.	D.	F'.	F".	Fx¹.	Fx².	K.	M.	N.	O.	F'.	F".	Fx.
1	161.6	....	....	165.	....	162.4	156.8	164.4	....	....	....	148.	....	135.8	....
1⅛	164.9	....	....	149.	162.8	168.8	141.2	157.	140.6	....	151.2	160.6	....	134.5	....
1¼	173.5	....	....	156.3	156.4	166.	162.	158.	131.4	178.4	151.4	155.6	158.8	106.8	165.2
1 5/16	....	....	....	....	....	....	....	....	....	....	....	....	149.	....	....
1⅜	170.3	....	....	158.	154.	164.2	154.2	158.6	150.6	140.	154.2	173.2	171.2	139.6	....
1 7/16	....	176.4	....	....	....	....	....	....	....	....	....	....	157.9	....	....
1½	167.5	....	161.9	170.8	160.2	167.6	161.8	161.6	141.2	157.2	162.8	170.	140.4	158.6	160.2
1⅝	155.6	....	155.5	104.8	162.5	164.6	152.4	160.8	149.7	127.3	164.2	160.6	....	169.4	169.9
1 11/16	....	166.7	....	....	....	....	....	....	....	....	....	....	....	....	....
1¾	173.	....	153.	158.6	166.9	157.8	142.8	151.2	124.1	....	161.8	177.6	....	163.	158.4
1 13/16	....	161.7	....	....	....	....	....	....	....	....	....	....	....	....	....
1⅞	176.	....	....	144.2	163.8	148.8	140.	156.4	160.	....	159.6	183.8	....	160.4	....
2	170.8	....	....	....	176.5	....	....	149.6	135.2	....	141.2	156.	....	....	....
Average	168.1	168.2	156.8	158.3	164.	162.5	151.4	157.5	141.6	150.7	155.8	165.7	155.5	153.5	163.9

Ratio of Strength of Sections of Links to that of the Bars from which they were made.

[CONSOLIDATED.]

Per Cent.	A.	B.	C.	D.	F¹.	F².	Fr¹.	Fx².	K.	M(1¼").	M(1⅜").	M(1½").	M(1¾").	N.	O.	P¹.	P².	Px.	Total.
Below 100 per cent	.	.	.	.	.	.	.	.	.	.	.	.	.	.	.	.	.	.	.
100 to 110 per cent	.	.	.	.	.	.	.	.	.	.	1	.	.	.	.	.	.	.	1
110 to 120 per cent	.	.	.	.	.	.	.	.	.	.	.	.	.	.	.	.	.	.	.
120 to 130 per cent	.	1	1	.	.	.	.	.	1	.	3	.	.	.	.	.	1	.	5
130 to 135 per cent	.	1	.	.	.	.	1	.	2	.	3	.	.	.	.	1	2	.	8
135 to 140 per cent	.	.	.	1	.	1	2	.	.	.	3	1	1	.	.	1	.	.	8
140 to 145 per cent	.	3	1	1	1	.	.	1	3	.	3	.	.	1	.	.	.	.	11
145 to 150 per cent	.	5	2	.	1	1	2	1	.	.	3	1	1	.	1	.	.	.	12
150 to 155 per cent	2	2	3	3	4	3	1	4	2	.	3	1	.	2	.	.	1	.	22
155 to 160 per cent	2	4	4	2	2	3	2	3	1	.	3	4	.	2	2	13	3	2	45
160 to 165 per cent	7	5	3	.	.	.	.	.	.	.	.	.	.	3	1	1	2	.	37
165 to 170 per cent	3	2	.	1	1	.	.	.	.	1	.	1	.	.	2	.	.	3	25
170 to 175 per cent	8	7	.	.	.	.	.	.	.	1	.	.	.	.	1	1	.	.	14
175 to 180 per cent	4	4	.	.	.	.	.	.	.	.	.	.	.	.	1	.	.	.	13
180 to 185 per cent	.	.	.	.	.	.	.	.	.	3	.	.	.	.	1	.	.	.	8
185 to 190 per cent	.	.	.	.	.	.	.	.	.	1	.	.	.	.	.	.	.	.	1
	26	34	14	8	9	8	8	9	9	6	22	8	2	8	9	16	9	5	210

We have the comparative records of 210 sections of cables broken by tension, which were made of fifteen different irons. Assuming that the utmost strength which can be found in a link is equal to 200 per cent of that of the bar from which it was made, we have a standard by which to compare the irons, and establish their relative value. Examining the abstracts by this standard, we find that 36 sections developed over 170 per cent of the bar's strength, 22 of them exceeded 175 per cent, 9 exceeded 180 per cent, and only one exceeded 185 per cent.

On the other hand, 67 sections developed less than 155 per cent, leaving 107, or over 50 per cent of the series, which developed between 155 and 170 per cent of the bar's strength; and of these the average development was 163 per cent.

The 210 sections of various irons can be reduced to 143 sections of iron which may be considered as more or less suitable for cable, by eliminating the records of the 67 sections, which were broken at less than 155 per cent of the bar's strength, and at once deciding that they have no claim to be considered as having been made from suitable chain-iron.

This we can do in many cases, and assign good reasons: 24 sections were made from an iron (M) in which analysis demonstrated that phosphorus, copper, nickel, and in some cases chromium, occurred, and possibly reduced their welding values, as all the "low breaks" of this iron occurred "through the weld;" eight were made from iron K, in which carbon was high, and ten from irons Fx and P, which were known to have been overworked, leaving but 22 such percentages to be assigned to the chapter of accidents. From which data we conclude that bars of fairly good chain-iron will produce links whose strength will not be less than 155 per cent, and not over 170 per cent; and that by a series of tests an average of not less than 163 per cent, made up of fairly uniform factors, should be expected.

We have therefore adopted for our standard of strength and welding qualities combined, 170 per cent of the strength of the bar for a maximum, 163 per cent for an average, and 155 per cent for a minimum. Iron which in the link form develops the average, by results which do not vary greatly, we consider to be *suitable;* that which falls below the average, or produces it by very irregular factors, we consider as *unsuitable.*

It remains to decide upon the strength of bar, which will most probably produce links which will develop the largest and most uniform percentages. Our records again supply the required data. We find the irons A, B, O, and F, which were low in tensile strength, sustained the process of manufacture into links with less loss of strength than did other irons which exceeded in this respect; and with all of the series excess of tensile strength was accompanied by deficiency in strength and uniformity as cable.

We have therefore decided upon adopting a *low tensile strength* as a probable indication of a *high welding* value, and as shown by the relative order as judged by the power of resisting sudden strains, of great resilience.

In selecting the low tensile strength, we did not decide arbitrarily in favor of the precedence which should be given to the percentage of bar's strength developed by the links. We find that in many cases the actual strength of the links made from the *bars* of low tensile strength equals and exceeds that of others from much stronger bars.

For example, iron K 2″ bar, tensile strength 58,900 pounds per square inch; strength of link, 258,900 pounds.

Iron A, tensile strength 2″ bar, 50,171 pounds; strength of link, 265,000 pounds.

Iron D, tensile strength 2″ bar, 51,152 pounds; strength of link, 276,500 pounds.

Iron F, tensile strength 2″ bar, 48,956 pounds; strength of link, 268,750 pounds.

In recommending for cable-manufacture iron of this character, we are aware that in so doing we will come in contact with a widely-spread and deeply-rooted prejudice in favor of the *strong bar* as best adapted to make *strong links.* It undoubtedly would be so, were it not that great strength in the direction of the fibre is not found often to exist except through the effect of a great amount of work, which will cause the iron to be too expensive for cable-iron, or through the presence of various chemicals which increase tenacity at the expense of welding properties, thus unfitting it for use as cable-iron.

We consider that our experiments justify us in recommending as a suitable strength for a 2″ bar of chain-iron a mean between the margins found to exist in those bars whose record both in bar and link form has been just given; and as the links of iron D, with tensile strength 51,152 pounds, and of iron F with 48,956 pounds, were equally good and strong, we adopt their mean of 50,000 pounds. And we find that iron A, which possesses nearly the medium strength as a bar (50,171 pounds), produces cable which is remarkably strong and uniform.

Considering, then, that an iron is suitable, which, as a 2″ bar, has strength of 50,000 pounds per square inch, and that other irons whose variation from this strength does not exceed five per cent above or three per cent below are equally suitable, we have, in determining the strength for the other sizes, to avail ourselves of the information procured in the investigation of the action of the rolls; which is, in brief, that the proportional strength of the bars of the same material increases as the diameter decreases, and that the aggregate of the increase for the sixteen sizes (measuring by sixteenths of an inch between 2″ and 1″) is from four to six thousand pounds, produced by steps which are made more or less irregular by irregularities in heating the piles.

Using the mean of the aggregate of increase of our best and most uniform irons, we find that the strength per square inch of a bar of 1″ diameter is about 5,600 pounds greater than that of the 2″, and that, if the 2″ bar is equal to 50,000 pounds, it is probable the 1″ will be equal to 55,600 pounds.

It was necessary to connect these strengths assigned to the extremes by a series of successively increasing factors, the aggregate of which should equal 5,600 pounds. It was evident that a uniform co-efficient of increase for each of the sixteen reductions could not be used, as the difference in strength produced by variations in reductions changed much less rapidly than did that

PROOF STRAINS FOR CHAIN-CABLES. 77

in the entire strength of the various-sized bars produced by variations in diameter. We therefore calculated a ratio which produced a constantly increasing co-efficient to be applied as the diameters decreased, with the results given in the table below; each of which results is the correction to be added to the strength per square inch of any size in order to obtain that of the size $\frac{1}{16}''$ less in diameter.

Starting with 50,000 pounds as the strength of the $2''$, and adding the increasing co-efficient, we arrive at a strength per square inch for each size which agrees closely with that found in the best and most uniform chain-irons. The latter, however, being exposed to constant chances of irregularities from many causes, cannot be expected to coincide in strength very closely with any calculated table.

Using the above factors of correction, we obtain the following table: —

Probable Strength of Round Bars, calculated with an Allowance for Variation in Strength due to Variation in Diameter.

Size of Bar.	Strength of Bar.			Size of Bar.	Strength of Bar.		
	Per Square Inch.	Coefficient of Increase.	Of Entire Bar.		Per Square Inch.	Coefficient of Increase.	Of Entire Bar.
	Pounds.	Pounds.	Pounds.		Pounds.	Pounds.	Pounds.
$2''$	50,000	245	157,080	$1\frac{7}{16}$	52,584	357	85,339
$1\frac{15}{16}$	245	253	148,137	$1\frac{3}{8}$	941	376	78,607
$1\frac{7}{8}$	498	262	139,430	$1\frac{5}{16}$	53,317	398	72,133
$1\frac{13}{16}$	760	273	130,066	$1\frac{1}{4}$	715	423	65,914
$1\frac{3}{4}$	51,033	284	122,745	$1\frac{3}{16}$	54,138	451	59,958
$1\frac{11}{16}$	317	296	114,770	$1\frac{1}{8}$	589	484	54,261
$1\frac{5}{8}$	613	309	107,040	$1\frac{1}{16}$	55,073	523	48,800
$1\frac{9}{16}$	922	323	99,560	1	596	. .	43,665
$1\frac{1}{2}$	52,245	330	92,322				

Accepting this rate of increase of strength as one which approximates to the actual increase of tenacity of iron bars of decreasing diameter, we have used it in the calculation of our proof-table.

A few examples will be given, which show conclusively that,

by means of the corrections for variation in diameter given in the table, the strength of a bar of, say, 2″, can be closely estimated from the data furnished by the test of 1″ bar. Selecting irons A, F, O, and P, which were quite uniform, the strength of the 2″ bars was: —

Actual strength...................A, 157,630 lbs.; F, 150,413 lbs.; O, 151,597 lbs.; P, 159,720 lbs.
Calculated with correction........A, 154,190 lbs.; F, 151,346 lbs.; O, 148,980 lbs.; P, 163,800 lbs.
Calculated without correction.....A, 161,830 lbs.; F, 163,136 lbs.; O, 166,635 lbs.; P, 181,600 lbs.

The latter process involving an *over-estimate* of from 12,700 to 24,200 pounds; which error is reduced in two cases by the use of the corrections to an over-estimate of 4,080 and 933 pounds, and in others to an under-estimate of 3,448 and 2,608 pounds.

The following table has been prepared, in which the average strength of such bars as have produced good cables is placed in contrast with the strength called for by the calculated table: —

Comparison of Calculated with Actual Strength of Bars.

Size of Bar.	Strength.		Difference.	Irons represented in Averages.		
	Calculated.	By actual Tests.		No. of Irons.	No. of Tests.	Name of Irons.
	Pounds.	Pounds.	Pounds.			
2″	157,080	157,580	500	9	35	A, C, D, E, F, Fx, M, O, P.
1 15/16	148,137	....	....	..	..	
1 7/8	139,430	141,120	1,690	9	26	Same as 2″.
1 13/16	130,966	131,975	1,009	5	8	B, C, E, G, H.
1 3/4	122,745	124,580	1,835	13	33	A, C, D, E, F, G, H, J, Fx, O, N, P, M.
1 11/16	114,770	115,690	920	4	7	B, C, E, G.
1 5/8	107,040	108,800	1,760	10	25	A, C, D, E, F, Fx, G, H, J, O.
1 9/16	99,560	....	....	..	..	
1 1/2	92,322	93,358	1,036	13	34	Same as 1½″.
1 7/16	85,339	85,000	339	6	12	B, C, E, G, H, P.
1 3/8	78,607	79,311	704	9	27	A, C, D, E, F, Fx, N, O, P.
1 5/16	72,133	74,505	2,372	1	94	P.
1 1/4	65,914	66,724	810	9	106	Same as 1⅜″.
1 3/16	59,958	....	....	..	..	
1 1/8	54,261	54,570	309	9	29	Same as 1⅜″.
1 1/16	48,800	....	....	..	..	
1	43,865	44,126	461	6	26	A, D, F, Fx, O, P.

PROOF STRAINS FOR CHAIN-CABLES. 79

Having thus fixed upon a suitable strength for each sized bar, we deduce the probable strength of cables made from them by the aid of the percentages of the bar's strength which we have found will probably be developed by the links, as indicated by those found in such irons as we have examined.

In this table of strength of links it is considered that no iron should be expected to possess in link form over 170 per cent of the bar's strength, and that no suitable chain-iron should possess less than 155 per cent of the same; and that the average strength of a number of tested sections should not be less than 163 per cent, such average to be made from fairly uniform factors.

Probable Strength of Cables made from Bars with Strength corresponding to that given in Table.

Size of Bar.	Strength of Entire Bar.	Maximum, 170 per cent of Bar.	Average, 163 per cent of Bar.	Minimum, 155 per cent of Bar.
	Pounds.	Pounds.	Pounds.	Pounds.
2″	157,080	267,036	256,040	243,474
1 15/16	148,137	251,833	241,463	229,612
1 7/8	139,430	237,031	227,271	216,116
1 13/16	130,966	222,642	213,475	202,997
1 3/4	122,745	208,666	200,074	190,255
1 11/16	114,770	195,109	187,075	177,894
1 5/8	107,040	181,968	174,475	165,912
1 9/16	99,500	169,250	162,283	154,318
1 1/2	92,322	156,947	150,485	143,099
1 7/16	85,339	145,076	139,103	132,275
1 3/8	78,607	133,632	128,129	121,841
1 5/16	72,133	122,626	117,577	111,806
1 1/4	65,014	112,054	107,440	102,167
1 3/16	59,958	101,029	97,731	92,935
1 1/8	54,261	92,244	88,445	84,105
1 1/16	48,800	82,960	79,544	75,640
1.	43,665	74,230	71,172	67,681

We have concluded that we cannot adopt a safer proof-strain than one which approximates to the *elastic limit* of the link; and the link whose elastic limit we should adopt is the *weakest* one which will, after proof, remain in the cable.

We have found by a great number of tests of bars in their

normal condition, that the elastic limit of good cable-iron is about 57 per cent of its ultimate strength.

The process by which the links are manufactured undoubtedly changes both the strength and elastic limit of the portion upon which the welds are made : the extent of this change we have no means of knowing; and so irregular are the processes of manufacture, that, if accurately ascertained in regard to a tested link, the data would be of no value in estimating its extent in the case of another.

We are therefore again reduced to probabilities. Generally the elastic limit of material is coincident with the first perceptible permanent change of form produced by stress. With a chain-link this cannot be accepted as correct, as, through various causes, the *form* of the link may change at a stress not great enough to produce change in the atomic relations of the material. Still, this first change of form *indicates* an approach to this limit; and we have carefully observed it in the test of many links, and find that with such irons as A, B, C, F, Px, and others considered suitable for cable, the percentage of the stress which will break the cable, at which the elongation can be observed and measured, is about 44 per cent, and that this percentage exists with considerable regularity, so much so that we feel justified in assuming it as the nearest approximation to the elastic limit of the link that can be deduced from our experiments. But we believe, for several reasons, that in most cases it is too low a percentage : first of which is, that, through badly fitting studs, many links during the beginning of an increasing stress may be considered as open or unstudded ones, and the "first stretch" is produced by a slight closure of the sides upon the stud; and open links begin to stretch at a much lower stress than studded ones. It is probable that a mean between the ratios of the ultimate strength at which the material in bar form begins to stretch, viz., 57 per cent, and that at which the links first elongate, viz., 44 per cent, will give as nearly the probable elastic limit of the link as can be obtained by any other process. No exact limit can be fixed upon.

PROOF STRAINS FOR CHAIN-CABLES. 81

We have, therefore, in calculating the proof-strains, assumed that it is not safe to use above 50 per cent of the strength of the weakest part of the cable.

The proving strains calculated upon the principles indicated are as follows: —

Recommended Proof-Table: being equal to 45.57 per cent of the Strength of the Strongest, and to 50 per cent of that of the Weakest, Links.

Size.	Proving Strain.		Size.	Proving Strain.	
Inches.	Pounds.	Tons.	Inches.	Pounds.	Tons.
2	121,737	$54\frac{777}{2240}$	$1\frac{7}{16}$	66,138	$29\frac{1178}{2240}$
$1\frac{15}{16}$	114,806	$51\frac{566}{2240}$	$1\frac{3}{8}$	60,920	$27\frac{440}{2240}$
$1\frac{7}{8}$	108,058	$48\frac{690}{2240}$	$1\frac{5}{16}$	55,903	$24\frac{2143}{2240}$
$1\frac{13}{16}$	101,499	$45\frac{699}{2240}$	$1\frac{1}{4}$	51,084	$22\frac{1804}{2240}$
$1\frac{3}{4}$	95,128	$42\frac{1048}{2240}$	$1\frac{3}{16}$	46,468	$20\frac{1568}{2240}$
$1\frac{11}{16}$	88,947	$39\frac{1587}{2240}$	$1\frac{1}{8}$	42,053	$18\frac{1733}{2240}$
$1\frac{5}{8}$	82,956	$37\frac{76}{2240}$	$1\frac{1}{16}$	37,820	$16\frac{1980}{2240}$
$1\frac{9}{16}$	77,159	$34\frac{999}{2240}$	1	33,840	$15\frac{240}{2240}$
$1\frac{1}{2}$	71,550	$31\frac{2110}{2240}$			

Comparison of the Proving Strains recommended, and Strains in Use.

Size of Cable.	Recommended Proving Strain.	Probable Percentage of Strength of —		Admiralty Proving Strain.	Probable Percentage of Strength of —	
		Strongest Link.	Weakest Link.		Strongest Link.	Weakest Link.
Inches.	Pounds.			Pounds.		
2	121,737	45.5	50	161,280	60.3	66.2
$1\frac{15}{16}$	114,806	45.5	50	151,357	60.1	65.9
$1\frac{7}{8}$	108,058	45.5	50	141,750	59.8	65.5
$1\frac{13}{16}$	101,499	45.5	50	132,457	59.4	65.2
$1\frac{3}{4}$	95,128	45.5	50	123,480	59.1	64.9
$1\frac{11}{16}$	88,947	45.5	50	114,817	58.8	64.5
$1\frac{5}{8}$	82,956	45.5	50	106,470	58.5	64.1
$1\frac{9}{16}$	77,159	45.5	50	98,437	58.2	63.7
$1\frac{1}{2}$	71,550	45.5	50	90,720	57.8	63.3
$1\frac{7}{16}$	66,138	45.5	50	83,317	57.4	62.9
$1\frac{3}{8}$	60,920	45.5	50	76,230	57.0	62.5
$1\frac{5}{16}$	55,903	45.5	50	69,457	56.6	62.1
$1\frac{1}{4}$	51,084	45.5	50	63,000	56.2	61.6
$1\frac{3}{16}$	46,468	45.5	50	56,857	55.7	61.1
$1\frac{1}{8}$	42,053	45.5	50	51,030	55.3	60.6
$1\frac{1}{16}$	37,820	45.5	50	45,517	54.8	60.1
1	33,840	45.5	50	40,320	54.3	59.5

The important points of difference between the recommended table and the one in use are: —

First, In the former, the proof stress is, for every size, uniform in its proportion to the probable strength of the links; in the latter, it varies with every change of size.

Second, Unless the elastic limit of the link is a greater proportion of its ultimate strength than that of the bar was of its strength, the strains of the table in use exceed this limit greatly, upon all sizes, while those of the former do not.

Third, The recommended table recognizes the probability of there being introduced into cables links made from bars which, although of equally good iron as the rest, are, through fault in rolling, more or less *scant*, and, in consequence, possess less strength than bars rolled true; which deficiency will be carried into the links. Should there, by accident, be a few links of $1\frac{15}{18}''$ in a $2''$ cable, the Admiralty proof would strain the strongest of such links to over 62 per cent, and the weakest to over 70 per cent, of the actual strength.

For these reasons we recommend that this table, based upon actual strength of American iron, be used in place of that of the Admiralty.

SECTION VII.

PART I. — *Notes upon the Various Irons examined, with Experiments showing Effects produced by reworking Material of Different Characteristics.* PART II. — *Chemical Analyses of the Irons, with Comparison of the Chemical and Physical Results.*

PART I.—NOTES UPON THE IRONS EXAMINED.

A COMPARISON of the results obtained by steady and sudden strains upon bars, and by steady strains upon the links made from the bars, indicates there are two classes of iron, which, although possessing considerable tensile strength in the form of straight bars, are equally unsuitable for cable-iron, through defective resilience, or inferior welding qualities.

The first class includes the greater portion of the ordinary cheap iron found in the market, which is cheap because it has not received enough work which is expensive, to greatly change its characteristics from those which it possessed as crude iron.

When tested by tension, iron of this class shows slight change of form at rupture; and when broken by impact it proves brittle and unreliable.

After fracture the appearance of the broken surface is described as "coarse granulous," and generally is bright and glistening.

Such iron will, when subjected to impact, break with but little deflection, and sometimes by blows of less force than it had previously withstood without sign of injury.

The second class includes many excellent irons with high tenacity, which is due either to very thorough work, or to ingredients in its composition which tend to increase tenacity, frequently at the expense of welding qualities.

A few notes in regard to the irons we have examined will illustrate these points.

CONTRACT CHAIN-IRON.

The general character of this iron was that of class first, coarse, brittle, and slightly worked.

As a result of the tests the entire stock on hand was condemned; but much of it having been found to be susceptible of great improvement by re-working, it was so treated with good results.

HAMMERED IRON.

The process by which this iron was manufactured was as follows:—

Such of the contract chain-iron as our experiments had shown to be most benefited by increased work was selected, heated to a very high heat, and thoroughly hammered by the steam-hammer, each link or bolt by itself, until it was flattened to a slab. During the process great quantities of dross and scoria were expelled.

Old condemned boilers were cut up, and the better portions cut into slabs, which were heated to a red heat, and the rust beaten off. These slabs of the two irons were then piled in the following manner:—

Boiler-iron.
Twice-hammered chain-iron.
Once-hammered chain-iron.
Crown-sheet boiler-iron.
Once-hammered chain-iron.
Twice-hammered chain-iron.
Boiler-iron.

These piles were about 20″ by 10″, and were heated and hammered into octagonal irons.

The advantages which it was hoped would be secured by the above method of piling were, that the soft and comparatively plastic centre would permit extreme flexure; that the coarse, once-heated chain-iron would, being supported by this yielding centre, sustain flexure to a much greater extent than if not so supported; and that the thoroughly re-heated and re-worked layers of chain-iron next to the outer layers would impart strength and toughness to the mass, and would absorb any blows or sudden strains, which received upon the outer surface would encounter first a cushion, and then a tough iron; and that the resultant iron would possess great power to resist both sudden and steady strains, would bend double without breaking, and, the parts not being perfectly homogeneous, the rupture of a portion of a bar would not render valueless the remainder. That we secured all these advantages, our tests show plainly.

Tested by tension, the iron showed fair tensile strength (average 53,000 pounds), uniformity, and ductility; tested by impact, bars of all sizes in their normal condition would sustain heavy blows with slight deflection, and finally double till the sides were close together, without injury. Extreme tests were made by impact: one hundred and ninety-seven bars of 2″ diameter were swaged from the blooms, each of which was circled with a score $\frac{1}{32}$ of an inch deep in the centre. These bars were struck upon this score by the wedge-shaped hammer of the impact testing machine, dropped from a height of thirty feet, the hammer weighing one hundred pounds. Each blow was considered to be equal to 3,000 foot-pounds.

2, or 1 per cent, resisted 7 blows.
5, or 2.54 per cent, resisted 6 blows.
27, or 13.6 per cent, resisted 5 blows.
68, or 34.5 per cent, resisted 4 blows.
71, or 36 per cent, resisted 3 blows.
21, or 10 per cent, resisted 2 blows.
3 broke at first blow.

The three which broke at single blow were found to have been made partially of boiler-steel.

Iron A.

From these hammered blooms, those which had resisted at least three blows were re-heated and rolled in the copper-mill into iron A.

All the bars showed great ductility and change of form under tension, having a rather low elastic limit, which was due, no doubt, to the fact that the softer and more ductile portions stretched first. Tested by impact, all sizes up to $2\frac{1}{4}''$ bent completely double by heavy blows (8,000 foot-pounds) delivered upon the centre of the test-pieces, bending them to the face of the wedge, when the steam-hammer completed the closure.

No iron which we have examined has proved superior to this for cable-iron; and there is no reason why any manufacturer should not be able to produce similar material, by suitable mixtures in the piles, and by giving such amount of work as is found to be best adapted to develop good welding properties.

Even though it should be considered as impractical to arrange every pile with due attention to a balancing of opposite characteristics, the quality of ordinary chain-iron can be vastly improved by subjecting the coarse material of which it is generally composed to much more thorough working than is ordinarily the custom.

Iron B.

Three bars of this iron, viz., $1\frac{3}{16}''$, $1\frac{11}{16}''$, and $1\frac{7}{16}''$, were furnished as sample bars to compete for an order for chain-iron, with bars of irons C, E, G, H, I, J, K, and L, all of which are referred to as the "nine irons." By the result of the tests, this iron was accepted for the three sizes, the contractor having substituted samples of iron B at the last moment for those of iron L previously furnished, which proved red-short and worthless. This iron showed plainly the effect upon quality of increased reduction by the rolls, the smaller sizes being the most ductile and welded most firmly.

Iron C.

Three bars of this iron, viz., 1¾", 1⅝", and 1½", were furnished to compete with the "nine irons;" and upon the results of the tests this iron was received in the above sizes.

The tests by tension and impact of the sample bars showed great ductility, low tensile strength, and remarkable toughness, with great power to resist impact.

As cable the welding value was high, and the single links developed from 178 per cent to 199 per cent of the bar's strength, averaging 187 per cent.

The iron delivered differed greatly from the samples: the tensile strength was higher; and, although generally tough and strong, the characteristics of the iron delivered showed that it had received much less work than the samples, if of the same material. As cable links the 1½" developed an average of 162 per cent, the 1⅝" 155 per cent, and the 1¾" 153 per cent, of the bar's strength, made up of very irregular factors, ranging from 134 to 177 per cent. The 1¾" was brittle under impact, the 1⅝" less so, and the 1½" generally very tough.

Iron D.

Two lots of this iron, each consisting of nine bars from 2" to 1", were purchased for testing. Differences in the amount of reduction in the rolls produced with this iron very marked differences in strength, — the smaller bars having much greater tenacity than the larger ones. All sizes possessed great power to resist impact, except the 2" bars, which were generally very brittle.

It seems probable that the second lot, having been prepared expressly for test, received a great deal more work than the first. This overwork manifested itself both in increased tenacity and in decreased welding value; the single links of the first lot developing an average of 178 per cent, and the sections of the second 158 per cent of the bar's strength.

The 2" bar of both lots differed greatly from all the smaller bars, — so greatly that it was difficult to believe that they were of the same iron. Both were very brittle under impact, and when tested by tension, broke with almost imperceptible change of form, showing bright granulous surface of fracture.

Iron E.

The iron was all of good quality, moderate tensile strength tough under impact, and made good cable.

This set of bars presented one peculiarity: the $1\frac{1}{2}''$, instead of being of less tensile strength than the $1\frac{5}{8}''$, as is generally the case, was of greater; and, on inquiry at the mill for the cause, we found that at this mill the pile used for the $1\frac{1}{2}''$ was of the same sectional area as that of the $1\frac{5}{8}''$, while at most mills it is less.

Iron F.

None of the bars furnished can be considered as chain-iron, for which purpose the manufacturers made a harder and stronger iron. We, however, tested many of them in the form of cables, considering that, in the records of such cables, we would find what could be expected of iron of very low tensile strength. F proved uniform under every form of test, the tensile strength, elongation, reduction of area, strength of links, and percentage of bar's strength developed by links, resistance to impact, and welding qualities, of any one lot, furnishing valuable evidence as to what might be expected of another.

Iron Fx.

The bars of this iron were rolled from piles made up of the same combination of crude irons as was used in the manufacture of iron F, but which piles were made to differ from those of F in sectional area.

The proprietors of the rolling-mill furnished, without charge, all the facilities and material necessary to assist the committee in an investigation into the effects of the rolls; the object of the experiments being the production of a set of bars, of various sizes, the tensile strength per square inch of which should be uniform.

This result was accomplished, on the third trial, by so graduating the sectional areas of the various piles, that the areas of the bars rolled from them bore uniform ratios to those of the piles. (See the record of this experiment, page 18.)

The resulting bars had received much more work than iron F: they had higher tenacity, equal if not superior resilience, but inferior welding qualities.

Irons G, H, I, and J.

These bars were furnished to compete with the nine irons for a contract, but few tests were made upon them.

G and H both proved of good fibrous material, sufficiently worked, and the few links made from them were strong; G, as single links, being equal to 174 per cent, and H to 182 per cent, of the bar's strength.

Iron I was thoroughly red-short; and it was impossible to make links from it, they breaking while being bent.

Six bars of iron J were furnished, which proved to be of a kind called in the shop "rotten." When tested by impact, with a sledge-hammer, the bars would split under the blows, showing smooth, black faces, resembling charcoal.

Iron K.

All the bars of this iron were of the same character, which was that of a fine-grained, thoroughly-worked, refined bar, of great tensile strength and uniformity, showing, when broken by any form of force, fine bright silvery fractures.

The bars were so uniform in strength that they were selected as the material from which to make experiments which depended upon uniformity in character of material for their value. Under impact-tests, iron K gave peculiar results: if the skin was intact, a bar of 2" diameter could be doubled, cold, by heavy blows, without showing injury; but if a slight score, or nick, was made in it, this power was entirely lost.

The welding properties were not good, that is, by the ordinary process. With some of the links, that were probably welded at suitable heat, the welds were firm, and they possessed great strength; but others, made from the same bars, broke at very low strains.

The character of the material was so opposite to that of charcoal-bloom boiler-iron, each possessing valuable qualities which were lacking in the other, that it was resolved to make some experiments by mixing the two; and the results show plainly, that, by such admixture, iron superior for chain-cables to either of the constituents could be produced, and that excellent chain-iron can be made by mills whose ordinary products cannot be considered as suitable.

Iron L.

Five bars were furnished to compete with the nine irons. All forms of test indicated that the material was steel; which analyses subsequently confirmed. The tensile strength was great; reduction of area abrupt; power of resistance to impact very slight when scored, but fair when not scored; welding-value low; strength of links very irregular.

Iron M.

A great number of tests were made upon this iron, both by physical and chemical processes. It was delivered as chain-iron at a number of different times and lots. The bars of these lots varied greatly among themselves; and the lots differed in many respects.

As cable, the iron proved very defective and irregular. The trouble with it seemed to be, that, if not welded at exactly the right heat (a very low one), the part of the link upon which the weld was made lost its strength by the process, and in many cases, when tested, the links would break through the weld at very low strains, showing little or no change of form, and the fractured ends remaining unreduced in diameter.

Iron N.

The bars of this iron (eight in number) were furnished to the committee by a leading manufacturer as samples of "first-class chain-iron;" and they were probably a fair sample of the ordinary character of such chain-iron: tested by tension, the strength was generally high, change of form slight.

Under impact, the large bars were very brittle, the 2" breaking by blows, when unscored, which the 1⅜" resisted after being scored. As cable, the 1⅜" was superior to the 2".

The fault with this iron was too little work, the large bars receiving much less than the small ones.

Iron O.

This iron is in no sense of the word a chain-iron; and its merits should not be judged by its action in the form of cable.

The material was soft charcoal-bloom, and of high price.

It proved of value in our experiments upon the effect of the rolls, and as furnishing us with data as to the extreme of change of form which would occur to a link of very soft iron under stress. Although too ductile and soft for chain-iron, some of the larger sizes produced good links, while the smaller sizes were overworked for the purpose, and did not.

Irons P and Px.

These irons were made at the same rolling-mill, and when the physical tests were made upon Px it was considered to be of the same material as P; and the differences in their characteristics were attributed to variations in the mechanical processes by which they were produced, P having received one course of heating and hammering which was omitted with Px. Subsequently chemical analyses showed marked differences in the nature of the two irons. The results of the analyses were confirmed by a letter from the manufacturer, in which he states that he perceives that the weak point of previous lots (iron P) was the lack of transverse strength when scored, and that he has in this lot (Px) overcome the difficulty, without essentially lowering the tensile strength. This was effected by, first, the selection and rigid puddling of pig-iron as free from phosphorus as possible; secondly, using a physic, which tended to eliminate the silicon and sulphur; and finally, the omission of the hammering. The result of these experiments by the manufacturer, to correct the defects found at the testing-machine, was the production of a superior chain-iron, which resisted impact well, and welded firmly.

PART II.— COMPARISON OF CHEMICAL AND PHYSICAL RESULTS.

Variations in the physical qualities of iron may be due to different composition, or to different treatment in manufacture, or to both of these complex causes. In order to determine the specific causes of variation, one class of altering conditions should be made to vary largely, while the other class should be kept uniform. Then another class should be varied, and so on until the value of each is ascertained. As all the irons under consideration were intended to have that purity and refinement which was deemed indispensable in chain-cables, their chemical analyses are, perhaps, more important in proving that physical variations result chiefly from variations in treatment, than in pointing out the specific effects of certain ingredients. While the subject of treatment — especially the increase of strength by greater reduction in rolling — may be the more important one, it can best be appreciated after we have familiarized ourselves with the general chemical and physical characters of the irons. The typical facts are given in the following tables: —

COMPARISON OF CHEMICAL AND PHYSICAL RESULTS.

TABLE I.—*Analyses of Irons used in making Chain Cables.*

Laboratory Number.	Iron and Size.	Sulphur.	Phosphorus.	Silicon.	Carbon.	Graphite.	Combined Carbon.	Manganese.	Copper.	Cobalt.	Nickel.	Slag and Oxide of Iron.	Chromium (Sol. in Dil. HCl.)	Chromium oxide (Insol. in Dil. HCl.)	SiO_2	Fe_2O_3	Cr_2O_3	CuO	MnO
135	A, 2"	0.007	0.178	0.139	0.021	0.009	0.012	0.031	0.172	0.068	0.078	1.210							
171	B, 1 7/8"	0.008	0.231	0.156	0.015			0.017	0.038	0.047	0.037								
172	C, 1 1/2"	0.007	0.169	0.154	0.042			0.021	0.046	0.029	0.031								
173	D, 1 1/4", lot 1	0.005	0.118	0.135	0.020			0.071	0.016	0.023	0.029								
186	D, 1", lot 1	0.009	0.191	0.185	0.045			0.097	0.012	0.023	0.026	0.546							
132	D, 1", lot 2	0.005	0.239	0.171	0.028	0.008	0.020	0.020	0.008	0.023	0.028	0.570							
174	D, 1 1/4", lot 2	0.005	0.158	0.108	0.024			0.038	0.018	0.031	0.026								
134	D, 2", lot 2, Nov. 1876	0.005	0.213	0.163	0.035	0.010	0.025	0.021	0.007	0.023	0.028	0.874							
175	E, 1 1/4"	0.013	0.181	0.159	0.018			0.021	0.054	0.044	0.042								
131	F, 1 1/4"	0.004	0.201	0.158	0.026	0.009	0.017	0.048	0.002	0.018	0.028	0.650							
169	Fx, 1 1/4", lot 1	0.004	0.187	0.163	0.032			0.031	0.010	0.026	0.013								
176	Fx, 1", lot 2	0.004	0.197	0.170	0.033			0.045	0.008	0.037	0.037								
177	Fx, 1 1/4", lot 3	0.004	0.193	0.170	0.028			0.039	0.006	0.042	0.042								
142	J, 1, 7/8"	0.003	0.140	0.182	0.027	0.007	0.020	Trace	0.004	Trace	0.008	1.120							
148	J, 1 1/8"	0.005	0.291	0.321	0.034	0.005	0.029	0.029	0.011	0.013	0.013	1.026							
143	J, 1 1/8"	0.005	0.213	0.295	0.035	0.007	0.028	0.029	0.009	0.003	0.008	0.678							
144	J, 1 1/2"	0.003	0.213	0.303	0.051	0.008	0.043	0.007	0.011	0.013	0.008	1.230							
137	J, 1 1/4"	0.004	0.154	0.257	0.033	0.008	0.025	0.053	Trace	Trace	0.013	1.724							
140	K	0.005	0.161	0.156	0.062	0.007	0.055	0.018	0.048	0.016	0.049	0.540							
130	K, 1 1/4"	0.004	0.161	0.169	0.099	0.010	0.059	0.026	0.079	0.027	0.034	0.470							
141	K, 1 1/4"	0.006	0.134	0.143	0.071	0.006	0.065	0.021	0.046	0.013	0.037	0.354							
136	L, 1 1/4"	Trace	0.065	0.105	0.453	0.024	0.429	0.006	0.008	Trace	0.011	0.326							
145	L, 1 1/8"	Trace	0.073	0.098	0.328	0.022	0.306	0.005	0.008	0.013	0.013	0.192							
146	L, 1 1/2"	Trace	0.067	0.098	0.512	0.016	0.496	0.029	0.010	0.010	0.016	0.308							

94 WROUGHT-IRON AND CHAIN-CABLES.

Analyses of Irons used in making Chain Cables.— Continued.

Laboratory Number.	Iron and Size.	Sulphur.	Phosphorus.	Silicon.	Carbon.	Graphic.	Combined Carbon.	Manganese.	Copper.	Cobalt.	Nickel.	Slag and Oxide of Iron.	Chromium (Sol. in Dil. HCl.)	Chromium oxide (Insol. in Dil. HCl.)	Si O	Fe₂ O₃	Cr₂ O₃	Cu₂ O	Mn O
138	L, 1 1/8"	Trace	0.074	0.080	0.212	0.013	0.199	0.014	0.006	0.010	0.013	0.452							
139	L, 1 3/8"	Trace	0.084	0.093	0.248	0.014	0.234	0.016	0.008	0.008	0.018	0.378							
184	L, 7/8"	0.001	0.089	0.103	0.229	....	....	0.019	0.007	0.015	0.018	0.383							
185	L, 7/8"	0.004	0.232	0.175	0.042	....	....	0.040	0.006	0.026	0.026	0.668							
155	M, 1 1/8"	0.003	0.248	0.174	0.026	0.012	0.014	Trace	0.314	0.110	0.340	1.096			0.022	0.990	0.160	None	
129	M, 1 3/8"	0.015	0.233	0.204	0.034	0.008	0.028	0.059	0.370	0.058	0.029	0.884			....	....	....	None	
147	M, 1 1/4"	0.007	0.317	0.259	0.039	0.005	0.034	0.021	0.374	0.098	0.175	1.034			0.040	0.716	0.316	None	A
133	M, 1 1/4"	0.008	0.219	0.159	0.063	0.007	0.056	0.022	0.328	0.052	0.039	0.674			....	....	....	None	
137	M, 1 1/4"	0.010	0.221	0.164	0.064	None	0.064	0.031	0.340	0.053	0.034	0.828			None	0.780	0.030	None	
158	M, 1 1/4", weld end	0.005	0.211	0.182	0.055	0.010	0.045	Trace	0.324	0.104	0.246	0.994	0.082	0.158	0.046	0.316	0.168	None	
159	M, 1 1/4", butt end	0.006	0.209	0.203	0.055	0.009	0.046	Trace	0.322	0.097	0.243	1.078	0.061	0.170	0.070	0.890	0.170	None	
160	M, 1 3/8", weld end	0.008	0.263	0.177	0.034	0.015	0.019	Trace	0.430	0.090	0.313	1.362	0.089	0.116	0.050	1.226	0.178	None	
161	M, 1 3/8", butt end	0.007	0.269	0.261	0.028	0.010	0.018	Trace	0.422	0.087	0.303	1.738	0.072	0.170	0.160	1.446	0.210	None	
213	M, 1 1/4"	0.010	0.207	0.173	0.036	....	....	0.013	0.320	0.079	0.236	1.616			0.068	1.408	0.130	None	0.007
212	M, 1 5/8"	0.017	0.125	0.138	0.003	....	....	0.117	0.092	0.026	0.023	0.590			0.060	0.442	0.032	Trace	0.041
211	M, 1 3/4"	0.002	0.195	0.154	0.045	....	....	0.013	0.442	0.000	0.026	1.182			0.028	1.133	0.012	None	0.012
210	M, 1 3/4"	0.005	0.238	0.155	0.032	....	....	0.014	0.370	0.055	0.026	0.720			0.010	0.678	0.050	0.001	Trace
214	M, 1 7/8"	0.011	0.166	0.187	0.053	....	....	0.012	0.408	0.047	0.026	0.994			0.076	0.992	Trace	Trace	0.004
215	M, 1 1/8"	0.010	0.247	0.180	.035	....	....	0.012	0.292	0.052	0.029	1.064			0.098	0.958	Trace	None	0.004
209	M, 2"	0.005	0.237	0.173	0.055	0.004	0.051	0.017	0.420	0.058	0.023	0.840			0.024	0.506	0.022	Trace	Trace
149	N, 1 1/4"	0.004	0.190	0.159	0.055	0.008	0.020	0.026	0.036	0.026	0.018	1.258			....	....	....	....	
150	N, 2"	0.006	0.192	0.169	0.028	0.007	0.038	0.050	0.028	0.031	0.028	2.202			....	....	....	....	
153	O, 1"	0.004	0.067	0.065	0.045	0.009	0.033	0.007	0.046	0.033	0.034	1.163			....	....	....	....	
154	O, 1 1/4"	0.005	0.078	0.073	0.042	0.008	0.025	0.005	0.046	0.034	0.037	0.974			....	....	....	....	
151	P, 1"	0.009	0.250	0.182	0.033	0.008	0.025	0.033	0.081	0.037	0.057	0.848			....	....	....	....	
152	Px, 1 1/4"	0.001	0.095	0.028	0.066	0.009	0.057	0.009	0.008	0.020	0.023	1.214			....	....	....	....	
156	Contract, 2 1/8"	0.046	0.328	0.238	0.026	None	0.026	Trace	0.134	0.039	0.042	0.768			None	0.716	0.040	None	....

COMPARISON OF CHEMICAL AND PHYSICAL RESULTS. 95

TABLE II.—*Relative Values of Iron in Bars in Tenacity, Reduction of Area, and Elongation, and in Proportion of Chain to Bar.*

ORDER OF VALUE.	TENSILE STRENGTH.		REDUCTION OF AREA.		ELONGATION.		PROPORTION OF TENACITY OF SHORT CHAIN TO THAT OF BAR.	
	Iron.	Pounds per Square Inch.	Iron.	Per Cent.	Iron.	Per Cent.	Iron.	Per Cent.
1	L	66,598	O	54.2	Px	29.9	B	168.2
2	K	58,050	A	49.0	E²	27.7	A	168.1
3	D¹	56,673	Px	48.9	P	23.2	O	165.7
4	C¹	56,001	F	48.1	O	22.7	Px	163.9
5	M	55,932	D¹	47.8	A	22.2	F	163.2
6	P	54,775	P	46.6	Fr³	22.0	D¹	158.3
7	N	54,329	Fr³	46.2	F	21.9	Fr³	157.5
8	Fr¹	54,271	E²	45.8	Fr¹	21.8	C¹	156.8
9	Px	54,091	Fr¹	45.3	M	21.0	N	155.8
10	D²	53,292	E²	45.0	D¹	20.9	P	154.5
11	Fr³	53,107	D²	43.8	N	20.2	Fr¹	151.4
12	B	52,764	C¹	40.6	D¹	18.2	M	150.7
13	A	52,579	M	38.2	C¹	18.0	K	141.6
14	E¹	52,583	C¹	38.1	K	17.9		
15	E²	52,471	K	38.0	B	17.2		
16	J	51,754	B	36.1	C¹	15.4		
17	F	51,153	N	33.0	E¹	15.3		
18	O	51,134	L	30.4	J	12.6		
19	C¹	50,765	J	25.9	L	8.3		

WROUGHT-IRON AND CHAIN-CABLES.

TABLE III. — Summary of the Principal Physical and Chemical Properties of Sixteen Irons.

Name of Iron.	L	K	D²	C¹	M	P	N	Fx¹	Fx	D¹	Fx³	B	A	J	F	O
	Per Cent.	Per Cent.	Per Cent.	Per Cent.	Per Cent.	Per Cent.	Per Cent.	Per Cent.	Per Cent.	Per Cent.	Per Cent.	Per Cent.	Per Cent.	Per Cent.	Per Cent.	Per Cent.
Number in tenacity	1	2	3	4	5	6	7	8	9	10	11	12	13	14	15	16
Number in reduction of area	15	12	9	11	10	8	14	8	3	5	7	13	2	10	4	1
Number in elongation	16	13	6	12	8	2	10	7	1	11	6	14	4	15	6	3
Number in welding value		13	6	8	12	10	9	11	4		1	1	2		5	3
Number in power of resisting shocks	14	12	6	7	11	9	13	3	7	9	2	9	1	14	4	4
Percentages of																
Phosphorus	0.072	0.152	0.203	0.169	0.225	0.250	0.191	0.187	0.095	0.154	0.193	0.231	0.178	0.292	0.201	0.072
Silicon	0.095	0.140	0.147	0.154	0.184	0.182	0.160	0.163	0.028	0.160	0.163	0.150	0.139	0.271	0.100	0.072
Carbon	0.350	0.008	0.020	0.042	0.044	0.033	0.055	0.032	0.006	0.033	0.032	0.015	0.021	0.036	0.020	0.043
Copper	0.009	0.058	0.011	0.046	0.353	0.081	0.032	0.010	0.008	0.014	0.006	0.038	0.172	0.009	0.002	0.040
Manganese	0.014	0.022	0.030	0.021	0.020	0.037	0.038	0.031	0.009	0.084	0.039	0.017	0.031	0.023	0.048	0.006
Cobalt	0.008	0.019	0.026	0.029	0.070	0.037	0.029	0.026	0.020	0.023	0.042	0.047	0.068	0.006	0.018	0.032
Nickel	0.014	0.040	0.027	0.031	0.132	0.057	0.023	0.013	0.023	0.028	0.042	0.037	0.078	0.010	0.028	0.031
Slag	0.331	0.455	0.722		1.044	0.848	1.760		1.214	0.540			1.210	1.156	0.050	1.071

NOTE. — The welding values of D¹, J, and L are omitted, as there were no short chains made from them. D¹ welded well, and J and L poorly. The percentages are averages when more than one analysis was made. Lab. Nos. 184, 185, 156, and 175 are omitted, there having been no short chains of these irons tested.

Table I. Analyses of the irons.

Table II. Relative values of irons in bars, in tenacity, reduction of area, and elongation, and in proportion of chain to bar.

Table III. Summary of principal physical and chemical characteristics of sixteen irons.

Under the head of phosphorus, the leading chemical and physical facts about each iron likely to be affected by this element are compared, and then the group of irons is considered, and a conclusion is reached; under the head of silicon, the irons are again gone over in a similar manner; and so on with carbon and other ingredients. A description of a few irons, in which composition should have the greatest influence on strength, will suffice to introduce these conclusions.

Effects of Phosphorus.

Iron **O**: P., 0.07; Si., 0.07; C., 0.04; slag, medium.
Chemical impurities all very low.
The iron had been thoroughly worked.
Tenacity as bar and as link very low.
Ductility as bar and as link very high.
Welds very good.
Low phosphorus does not alone account for these qualities. Iron **F**, with P. 0.20, Si. 0.16, and C. 0.03, has about the same tenacity and welding power, and approaches the same ductility. Iron **P**, with P. 0.25, Si. 0.18, and C. 0.083, has about equal ductility, but inferior welding qualities. Seeing that the thorough working of the small bars decreased welding power, as compared with that of the less compressed large bars, it is probable that method of manufacture is an important factor in all physical results. The effects of low phosphorus are not conspicuous.

Iron **P**: P., 0.25; Si., 0.18; C., 0.03; slag, very low.
P., rather high; C., medium; other impurities, low.
Tenacity high as bar, irregular as link.
Ductility high when not nicked, low when nicked. Welding value medium, through overwork, and possibly high P.

Iron **Px**: P., 0.09; Si., 0.028; C., 0.066.

This iron had the highest average of good qualities of the commercial bars examined, and was the best for general construction purposes. The characteristic effects of phosphorus might, previous to our investigation into the effects of reduction, have been considered as shown by the behavior of two specimens, one of iron **P**, and one of **Px**, made in the same way, except that one course of piling and hammering was omitted from **Px**; viz., —

1″ bar-iron **P**: phosphorus, 0.25; tenacity, 57,807 pounds; elongation, 19 per cent.

1¾″ bar-iron, **Px**: phosphorus, 0.09; tenacity, 54,212 pounds; elongation, 24 per cent.

But this increased tenacity and decreased ductility of the smaller bar are not due to P. alone: it had Si. 0.18 against Si. 0.03, and it had more reduction in the rolls.

The difference in the tenacity of the bars of the same sizes of iron **P**, which may be considered as probably of similar composition, was nearly 5,000 pounds; while between the bars in question, **P** and **Px**, it was but 3,600 pounds.

Phosphorus may have affected the welding qualities and the ductility; as iron **Px**, with much less of this element, welded much better, and had greater powers of resisting sudden strains, than iron **P**.

Iron **D**: P., 0.18 (0.12 to 0.24); Si., 0.15; C., 0.03 · slag, low.

Carbon low, other impurities medium.
Different bars very differently worked.
Tenacity high as bar and link.
Ductility medium as bar and link.
Welds very good.

There are various proofs that low phosphorus, even with low silicon, does not cause high ductility, and that the amount of reduction is the more important factor. For instance: —

1″ bar, P. 0.24, Si. 0.17, has tenacity per square inch, 61,000 pounds; elongation, 26 per cent.

1½" bar, P. 0.16, Si. 0.11, has tenacity per square inch, 56,000 pounds; elongation, 23 per cent.

2" bar, P. 0.21, Si. 0.16, has tenacity per square inch, 49,146 pounds; elongation, 0.07 per cent.

The welds of the medium-sized and worked bars are the best, but all were good. No harmful effects of phosphorus can be traced in this iron.

Iron **B** welded best, and had P. 0.23, and C. 0.015.

Iron **F**: P., 0.20; Si., 0.16; C., 0.03; slag, low.

Carbon low, other impurities medium.

Iron suitably worked for welding, and very uniform.

Tenacity as bar and as link very low.

Ductility high.

Welding power good.

The remarkable uniformity of this iron proves it to have been made with great care, from selected materials. Why its tenacity is so low, it is difficult to say, on chemical grounds. The same iron, **Fx**, more worked, gives a medium tenacity, with substantially the same analysis. Iron **A**, with less P., Si., and C., is stronger. Iron **E** has lower P., the same Si., and only 0.02 C., and yet a higher tenacity.

Iron **Fx** (**F** more worked): P., 0.19; Si., 0.17; C., 0.03.

Ingredients substantially the same as in **F**.

Iron much more worked than **F**.

Tenacity medium in link and bar.

Ductility good.

Welding power below medium.

Iron **B**: P., 0.23; Si., 0.16; C., 0.015.

P. rather high, Si. medium, and C. very low.

Iron not sufficiently worked for strength.

Tenacity rather low.

Ductility quite low.

Welds very good.

Notwithstanding the extremely low C., the iron was not ductile. P. may well account for this, but not for low tenacity, as some of iron **P** had more P., and much higher tenacity. Low

C. may partly account for low tenacity and good welds, but small reduction seems to be an equal cause. High P. did not prevent excellent welding.

Iron **M**: P., 0.25 (0.21 to 0.32); Si., 0.18 (0.16 to 0.26); C., 0.04; Ni., 0.18 (0.03 to 0.34); Cu., 0.34 (0.13 to 0.43); slag, various.

P. rather high, Si. above medium, copper and nickel high, C. rather low.

The amount of work the iron received can only be inferred from the sizes of the bars.

Tenacity considerably above average.

Ductility average.

Welds weak.

The character of this iron is so complex, and its physical character varies so much in the same-sized bars, that no satisfactory analysis of the data can be made. It seems certain from a comparison of the tables, that neither copper, nickel, cobalt, nor slag materially affected strength. The effects of these ingredients on welding will be considered under another head.*

Conclusions about Phosphorus. — The best of these irons average P. 0.09 to 0.20. The extreme limits are 0.065 and 0.317. A soft boiler-plate steel might have the former amount: the latter would give high tenacity and brittleness to even a low carbon steel. The investigations have been made so difficult by the chemical similarity and general purity of most of the irons, and by their various degrees of reduction in rolling, that the effects of phosphorus cannot be independently traced.

The phosphorus (average in each iron) runs very irregularly as follows, beginning with the highest of the following physi-

---

* Chromium occurs only in iron M, four analyses of which show, Cr. 0.061 to 0.089. As this element is known to increase the tenacity of steel, it may have brought iron M up to a good standard of tenacity without helping its other stuctural qualities. These experiments give no absolute evidence as to the effects of chromium; but it may be said that when mere tenacity is made the criterion of fitness, an iron like M may be found which will meet *that* requirement, and still prove untrustworthy for cables.

cal values: *Tenacity*, 0.72, 0.15, 0.20, 0.17, 0.22, 0.25, 0.19, 0.19, 0.09, 0.15, 0.19, 0.23, 0.18, 0.20, 0.20, 0.07. *Reduction of Area*, 0.07, 0.18, 0.09, 0.20, 0.15, 0.25, 0.19, 0.19, 0.20, 0.22, 0.17, 0.15, 0.23, 0.19, 0.07, 0.20. *Elongation*, 0.09, 0.25, 0.07, 0.18, 0.19, 0.20, 0.19, 0.22, 0.20, 0.19, 0.15, 0.17, 0.15, 0.23, 0.20, 0.07.

It may be generally stated that phosphorus 0.10, with carbon about 0.03, and silicon under 0.15, gave the best chain-cable irons of this group. One of the best irons, however, had P. 0.23, although low tenacity and high ductility are the chief requirements of such irons.

The effects of the different constituents on welding will be considered under that head.

EFFECTS OF SILICON.

See foregoing description, of irons **O**, **P**, **F**, and **M**.

In iron **F**, which is among the highest in silicon, did this element cause the very low tenacity despite the fair amount of P. (0.20)? If so, Si. must affect tenacity more than it affects ductility. But this is not the fact. In iron **J**, ductility as well as tenacity is made very low by high Si. (0.27).

Iron **J**: Si., 0.27 (0.18 to 0.32); P., 0.20; C., 0.035; slag, average.

Silicon high, other impurities medium.
Iron not overworked.
Tenacity very low in bar and link.
Ductility very low in bar and link.
Weld rather bad.

There was no apparent chemical or physical cause for this low strength, except excessive silicon. Under sledge-blows the bars split as often as they broke off; and the faces of the fracture were like layers of charcoal, although both carbon and slag were medium.

Conclusions about Silicon. — No ingredient of *steel* is less understood than this one. The technical managers of the Terrenoire Works in France, who have been notably successful in their steel manufactures founded on chemical induction, especially in the manufacture of sound steel castings which contain a large amount of Si., believe that this ingredient, up to the amount contained in most of the irons we are considering, does not decrease the tenacity or ductility of steel. And it is true that good steels are made by various processes with as much as 0.20 Si. It is believed by the Terrenoire managers that silica is the cause of the bad effects usually attributed to silicon. The table of analyses will show that in this case the ore has not been mistaken for the metal. The slag, which contains the silica, has been separately determined. Why wrought-iron should differ from steel in respect of the effects of Si., we have not so far been able to determine, if, indeed, it does so differ. It can only be said, with reference to this series of experiments, that there is an apparent decrease of strength due to an excess of this element, while the effects of medium amounts of it are overshadowed by larger causes. The extremes of Si. were 0.028 and 0.321. In the best irons it averaged about 0.15. It ran as follows, with a regularly decreasing order of value: In *Tenacity*, Si., 0.09, 0.15, 0.15, 0.15, 0.18, 0.18, 0.17, 0.16, 0.03, 0.16, 0.16, 0.16, 0.14, 0.27, 0.16, 0.07. *Reduction of Area*, Si., 0.07, 0.14, 0.03, 0.16, 0.16, 0.18, 0.16, 0.16, 0.15, 0.18, 0.15, 0.15, 0.16, 0.17, 0.09, 0.27. *Elongation*, Si., 0.03, 0.18, 0.07, 0.14, 0.16, 0.16, 0.16, 0.18, 0.15, 0.17 0.16, 0.15, 0.15, 0.16, 0.27, 0.09.

EFFECTS OF CARBON.

See foregoing remarks on iron **B**, in which C. is extremely low.

Iron **L**: C., average 0.35, highest 0.51; P., 0.10; Si., 0.10; slag, low.

Carbon very high, other impurities quite low.

Tenacity as bar highest.

Ductility as bar and link lowest.

Welding power most imperfect, decreasing as C. increases.

The following table,* from a paper by William Hackney,

* Read before the Institution of Civil Engineers, London, April, 1875.

Esq., is valuable in this connection, as showing the amounts of C. in various well-known brands of wrought iron and steel.

Percentages of Carbon in some Varieties of Iron and Steel.

SERIES OF THE IRONS.		SERIES OF THE STEELS.	
Description.	Percentage of Carbon.	Description.	Percentage of Carbon.
Soft puddled iron	Trace.*	Extra soft Fagersta Bessemer steel	0.085 §
Armor plates	{ 0.016 † { 0.033 † { 0.044 †	Extra soft Dowlais Bessemer steel	0.135 ‖
Iron rail	0.09 ‡	Crews boiler-plate steel, Bessemer process	0.22 to 0.24 ¶
Lowmoor boiler-plate	0.10 ‡		
Staffordshire boiler-plate	0.19 †	Locomotive crank-axles, Sera-ing Bessemer steel	0.31 ‡ 0.49 ‡
Russian bar-iron	{ 0.272 † { 0.340 †	Locomotive crank-axle, by Vickers, Sheffield	0.46 *
Swedish iron bar	{ 0.054 † { 0.097 † { 0.386 †	Rails and tires	0.30 to 0.50
		Bessemer spring steel	0.45 to 0.55 ‡
Steely puddled iron	0.30 to 0.40 ‡	Crucible steel:	
Iron made by Catalan process direct from the ore	{ traces.† { 0.420 †	For masons' tools	0.6 *
		For chipping chisels	0.75 *
Soft puddled steel	0.501 †	Crank-axle (by Krupp)	1.05 ‡
Puddled steel rail	0.55 ‡	Gun (by Krupp)	1.18 †
Hard puddled steel	1.380 †	For flat files	1.20 *
		Forged Indian wootz	1.645 †

Iron **L** is, therefore, a so-called puddled steel, or more properly a weld-steel. Since its impurities, other than C., are so small, it is impossible to avoid the conclusion that C. is the cause of its marked physical character. This is more plainly shown by the following: —

1½ in. bar, C. 0.45, has nearly 70,000 pounds tenacity per square inch, and 6.5 per cent elongation.

1⅜ in. bar, C. 0.51, has 67,000 pounds tenacity per square inch, and 6.5 per cent elongation.

1 11/16 and 1 7/8 in. bar, C. 0.21 to 0.25, have average 58,000 pounds tenacity per square inch, and 13 per cent elongation.

Iron **K**: C., 0.07; P., C.15; Si., 0.15; slag, low.
C. slightly high, other impurities medium.
Iron well worked and very uniform.
Tenacity as bar and link very high.

* A. Willis. † J. Percy. ‡ A. Greiner.
§ D. Forbes. ‖ Snelus. ¶ F. W. Webb.

Ductility below medium.
Welding power quite low.
The ductility was very fair when the bar was not nicked. The fracture was fine and silvery, like that of low steel. These facts, and the medium amounts of other impurities, point to C. as the hardening element. Irons having similar amounts of P. and Si., and low carbon, like irons **A** and **C**, have lower tenacity and higher ductility.

Iron **E**: C., 0.018; P., 0.18; Si., 0.16.
C. very low, other impurities medium.
Tenacity below average.
Ductility high.
Welding power pretty good.
These phenomena seem to be connected with low carbon.

Conclusions about Carbon. — So much is known concerning the influence of C. on both wrought-iron and steel, that there is little danger of falling into error about it. The irons under consideration have C. almost exclusively low and pretty uniform: the exceptional cases give very marked physical results, especially iron **L**, which is the only one really high in C. · The other irons ranged between 0.015 and 0.07. Carbon ran with the following decreasing order of value in *Tenacity:* C. 0.35, 0.068, 0.032, 0.042, 0.044, 0.033, 0.055, 0.032, 0.066, 0.032, 0.032, 0.015, 0.02, 0.036, 0.026, 0.043. *Reduction of Area,* 0.043, 0.02, 0.006, 0.026, 0.032, 0.033, 0.032, 0.032, 0.032, 0.044, 0.042, 0.068, 0.015, 0.055, 0.35, 0.036. *Elongation,* 0.066, 0.033, 0.043, 0.02, 0.032, 0.026, 0.032, 0.044, 0.032, 0.055, 0.032, 0.042, 0.068, 0.015, 0.036, 0.35.

It seems thus easy to vary the physical qualities of puddled iron by carbon; but whether or not it is easy to *uniformly* vary the carbon in puddled iron, the checkered history of the "puddled-steel" process will show. As we shall observe farther on, for uses in which the value of an iron depends on the strength of the particular kind of weld given to these links, C. must be under 0.04. But for uses in which the strength of the bar is the measure of fitness, C. may run up to 0.50 or more.

COMPARISON OF CHEMICAL AND PHYSICAL RESULTS. 105

Manganese is so very low in all these irons, that its effects cannot be traced. It is highest in one lot of iron **D**, viz., 0.097; but even this could have little effect, in view of the fact that Mn. is often three times as high in very soft steels, and sometimes runs above one per cent in low structural steels. Mn. seems to toughen steel, and to make it cast sound: its hardening effect up to Mn. 0.20 to 0.30 is slight.

Copper is very low in all the irons, except **M** (Cu. 0.31 to 0.43), which has about the average tenacity and ductility. Cu. is next highest (Cu. 0.17) in iron **A**, which has rather low tenacity, but very high ductility, on account of its low carbon (C. 0.02). These experiments furnish no evidence that copper affects strength. Its effect on welding will be further considered.

Nickel was only high (Ni. 0.34) in some of the bars of iron **M**, but did not appear to affect their strength. That it may have helped their welding capacity, is further referred to.

Cobalt was so low (Co. 0.11 maximum) that its effects on strength could not be traced. Possibly copper may have been neutralized by Ni. and Co. in its effect on strength, but these data are not evidence one way or the other.

Sulphur was extremely low in all the irons, S. 0.046 being the highest percentage in one lot of iron **M**. So little S. did not affect welding power, as we shall observe farther on; and it could hardly impair strength, when irons red-short from much S. are usually strong.

Slag. — This averages about one per cent. It is lowest in iron **L** (slag 0.38), and highest in the 2″ bar of iron **N** (slag 2.26). This bar had 51,700 pounds tenacity, and 8.7 per cent elongation; while the 1⅛″ bar of iron **N**, with 1.258 slag, had 56,000 pounds tenacity, and 21.7 per cent elongation. Was this the result of too little work on the larger bar, or of the slag *per se?* Is the presence of much slag merely an indication of too little work, — of a loose structure resulting from too little condensation of the fibres? Or does the slag, as slag, or dirt, exert an independent weakening influence? Referring to the table of analyses we find: —

Iron.	Size.	Slag.	Iron.	Size.	Slag.
L . . .	$\tfrac{5}{8}''$	0.668	O . .	$1\tfrac{1}{4}''$	1.096
L . . .	$\tfrac{7}{8}''$	0.388	O . .	$1\tfrac{1}{2}''$	0.974
L . . .	$1\tfrac{1}{16}''$	0.192	P . .	$1''$	0.848
L . . .	$1\tfrac{1}{8}''$	0.326	P . .	$1\tfrac{3}{4}''$	1.214
L . . .	$1\tfrac{3}{8}''$	0.308	D . .	$1''$	0.570
L . . .	$1\tfrac{11}{16}''$	0.452	D . .	$2''$	0.546
L . . .	$1\tfrac{13}{16}''$	0.376			

It appears that the smallest and most worked iron often has the most slag. It is hence reasonable to conclude that an iron may be dirty and yet thoroughly condensed; and it therefore seems probable that the $1\tfrac{1}{4}''$ bar of iron **N** was 4,300 pounds stronger than the $2''$ bar, partly because it had one per cent less slag. The $1''$ bar of iron **P** had nearly 58,000 pounds tenacity; while the $1\tfrac{3}{4}''$ bar of **Px**, with 0.40 more slag, had a little less than 53,000 pounds tenacity. It is, however, impossible to establish any close conclusions from these small variations of slag. The investigation requires analyses of irons equally worked, some of the specimens being purposely made very dirty.

WELDING.

Before comparing the irons under this head, it may be well to briefly consider the heretofore ascertained facts, and the speculations which grow out of them. The generally received theory of welding is, that it is merely pressing the molecules of metal into contact, or rather into such proximity as they have in the other parts of the bar. Up to this point there can hardly be any difference of opinion, but here uncertainty begins.

What impairs or prevents welding? Is it merely the interposition of foreign substances between the molecules of iron and any other substance which will enter into molecular relations or vibrations with iron? Is it merely the mechanical preventing of contact between molecules, by the interposition of such substances? This theory is based on such facts as the following: —

1. Not only iron, but steel, has been so perfectly united that the seam could not be discovered, and that the strength was as great as it was at any point, by accurately planing and thoroughly smoothing and cleaning the surfaces, binding the two pieces together, subjecting them to a welding heat, and pressing them together by a very few hammer-blows. But when a thin film of oxide of iron was placed between similar smooth surfaces, a weld could not be effected.

2. Heterogeneous steel-scrap, having a much larger variation in composition than these irons have, when placed in a box composed of wrought-iron side and end pieces laid together, is (on a commercial scale) heated to the high temperature which the wrought-iron will stand, and then rolled into bars which are more homogeneous than ordinary wrought-iron. The wrought-iron box so settles together as the heat increases, that it nearly excludes the oxidizing atmosphere of the furnace, and no film of oxide of iron is interposed between the surfaces. At the same time the enclosed and more fusible steel is partially melted; so that the impurities are partly forced out, and partly diffused throughout the mass, by the rolling.

The other theory is, that the molecular motions of the iron are changed by the presence of certain impurities, such as copper and carbon, in such a manner that welding cannot occur or is greatly impaired. In favor of this theory it may be claimed that, say, two per cent of copper will almost prevent a weld; while, if the interposition theory were true, this copper could only weaken the weld two per cent, as it could only cover two per cent of the surfaces of the molecules to be united. It is also stated that one per cent of carbon greatly impairs welding power, while the mere interposition of carbon should only reduce it one per cent.

On the other hand, it may be claimed that in the perfect welding due to the fusion of cast-iron, the interposition of ten or even twenty per cent of impurities, such as carbon, silicon, and copper, does not affect the strength of the mass as much as one or two per cent of carbon or copper affects the strength of a weld made at a plastic instead of a fluid heat. It is also true that high tool steel, containing one and a half per cent of carbon, is much stronger throughout its mass, all of which has been welded by fusion, than it would be if it had less carbon. Hence copper and carbon cannot impair the welding power of iron in any greater degree than by their interposition, provided the welding has the benefit of that *perfect mobility* which is due to fusion. The similar effect of partial fusion of steel in a wrought-iron box has already been mentioned. The inference is, that imperfect welding is not the result of a change in molecular motions, due to impurities, but of imperfect mobility of the mass, — of not giving the molecules a chance to get together.

Should it be suggested that the temperature of fusion, as compared with that of plasticity, may so change chemical affinities as to account for the different degrees of welding power, it may be answered that the temperature of fusion in one kind of iron is lower than that of plasticity in another, and that, as the welding and melting points of iron are largely due to the carbon they contain, such an impurity as copper, for instance, ought, on this theory, to impair welding in some cases, and not to affect it in others. This will be further referred to.

The next inference would be, that by increasing temperature we chiefly improve the quality of welding. If temperature is increased to fusion, welding is practically perfect; if to plasticity and mobility of surfaces, welding should be nearly perfect.

Then, how does it sometimes occur, that, the more irons are heated, the worse they weld?

1. Not by reason of mere temperature; for a heat almost to dissociation will fuse wrought-iron into a homogeneous mass.

2. Probably by reason of oxidation, which, in a smith's fire especially, necessarily increases as the temperature increases. Even in a gas-furnace, a very hot flame is usually an oxidizing flame. The oxide of iron forms a dividing film between the

surfaces to be joined; while the slight interposition of the same oxide, when diffused throughout the mass by fusion or partial fusion, hardly affects welding. It is true that the contained slag, or the artificial flux, becomes more fluid as the temperature rises, and thus tends to wash away the oxide from the surfaces; but inasmuch as any iron, with any welding flux, can be oxidized till it scintillates, the value of a high heat in liquefying the slag is more than balanced by its damage in burning the iron.

3. But it still remains to be explained, why some irons weld at a higher temperature than others; notably, why irons high in carbon, or in some other impurities, can only be welded soundly by ordinary processes at low heats. It can only be said that these impurities, as far as we are aware, increase the fusibility of iron, and that in an oxidizing flame oxidation becomes more excessive as the point of fusion approaches. Welding demands a certain condition of plasticity of surface: if this condition is not reached, welding fails for want of contact due to mobility; if it is exceeded, welding fails for want of contact due to excessive oxidation. The temperature of this certain condition of plasticity varies with all the different compositions of irons. Hence, while it may be true that heterogeneous irons, which have different welding-points, cannot be soundly welded to one another in an oxidizing flame, it is not yet proved, nor is it probable, that homogeneous irons cannot be welded together, whatever their composition, even in an oxidizing flame. A collateral proof of this is, that one smith can weld irons and steels which another smith cannot weld at all, by means of a skilful selection of fluxes and a nice variation of temperatures.

To recapitulate: It is certain that perfect welds are made by means of perfect contact due to fusion, and that nearly perfect welds are made by means of such contact as may be got by partial fusion in a non-oxidizing atmosphere or by the mechanical fitting of surfaces, *whatever* the composition of the iron may be within all known limits. While high temperature is thus the first cause of that mobility which promotes welding, it is also the cause, in an oxidizing atmosphere, of that "burning" which injures both the weld and the iron. Hence, welding in an oxidizing atmosphere must be done at a heat which gives a compromise between imperfect contact due to want of mobility on the one hand, and imperfect contact due to oxidation on the other hand. This heat varies with each different composition of irons. It varies because these compositions change the fusing-points of irons, and hence their points of excessive oxidation. Hence, while ingredients such as carbon, phosphorus, copper, &c., positively do not prevent welding under fusion, or in a non-oxidizing atmosphere, it is probable that they impair it in an oxidizing atmosphere, not directly, but only by changing the susceptibility of the iron to oxidation.

The obvious conclusions are: 1st, That any wrought-iron, of whatever ordinary composition, may be welded to itself in an oxidizing atmosphere at a certain temperature, which may differ very largely from that one which is vaguely known as "a welding heat." 2d, That in a non-oxidizing atmosphere, heterogeneous irons, however impure, may be soundly welded at indefinitely high temperatures.

These speculations may throw little light on the subject of welding. They are introduced for the purpose of indicating the direction of further inquiry and experiment, and of impressing the necessity of caution in arriving at conclusions about these irons from the limited data afforded by these experiments.

In reviewing the experiments with reference to welding, and under the precaution mentioned, let us observe:—

1st, All the irons were so very low in sulphur, that this ingredient could not have materially affected welding power.

2d, As we shall see in detail, farther on, the irregular differences in the working and reduction of the bars, which affected all other physical properties, affected this one also.

Let us first take the singularly impure iron **M**. Its surfaces were pretty well united by welding, but the iron about the weld was weakened, especially at a high heat. Of 124 ruptures of links made of this iron, 79 were through the weld, and the iron was little distorted. Of 311 ruptures of links made of other irons, but 37 were through the weld.

The 1¼″ bar of iron **M** presents an exception: it stands high on the list in welding capacity, and contains copper 0.31 (average Cu. in iron **M**, 0.34). Its phosphorus, slag, and silicon are about average. But the bar is also remarkable in containing nickel 0.35, and cobalt 0.11. Did these ingredients neutralize the copper under this special treatment? No other irons contain any notable amount of them, except iron **A**, which has Co. 0.07, and Ni. 0.08; but it also has Cu. 0.17.* The welds of this iron were very strong, the links breaking oftener at the butt than at the weld.

Two links made from iron **M** were analyzed from specimens taken at the weld end and at the butt end. The weld end had been re-heated and hammered twice; the butt end had not been hammered, and had received second heat only by conduction from the other end. The analyses show that silicon and slag only were materially affected by twice heating and hammering, as follows:—

	Silicon.	Slag.
Iron M, 1½ in. bar, weld end	0.182	0.998
" 1½ in. bar, butt end	0.203	1.074
" 1⅜ in. bar, weld end	0.177	1.388
" 1⅜ in. bar, butt end	0.261	1.732

In oxidizing to silica, the Si. diffused a small amount of flux, which should have helped welding by preventing oxidation, or by carrying off oxide of iron, or both; but the amount was so very small in this case that its effect cannot be traced. Nor does iron **J**, in which Si. was highest (0.18 to 0.32), confirm

---

* This iron may have received the copper while being rolled in a train ordinarily used for copper, at the Navy Yard, Washington, D.C., where it was manufactured.

this theory. Although the other impurities were not high, and the iron was not overworked, it welded rather badly. The value of short chains is as follows: Best, Si. 0.16, 0.14, 0.07, 0.03, 0.16, 0.15, 0.17, 0.15, 0.17, 0.18, 0.16, 0.18, 0.15, and, including **J**, 0.27.

Phosphorus, up to the limit of ¼ per cent, had not a notable effect on welding. It was lowest in iron **O**, which welded soundly; but all impurities were low, and welding power was traced to the reduction of the bar by direct experiment. The same is true of iron **P**. Omitting one course of piling and hammering largely helped its welding power. Iron **P** welded badly, not necessarily on account of its P. 0.25; for iron **B**, with P. 0.23, and iron **D**, with P. 0.18, welded soundly. Iron **M** had the high P. 0.23 (0.21 to 0.32). While its surfaces stuck together pretty well, the links broke through the weld when they were made at a high heat, which may be accounted for by the fact that phosphorus increases fluidity, and hence capacity for oxidation. The value of short chains is in the following order: Best, P. 0.23, 0.18, 0.07, 0.09, 0.20, 0.20, 0.19, 0.17, 0.19, 0.25, 0.19, 0.22, 0.15.

Carbon notably affected welding. It ran as follows in connection with regularly decreasing welding power: Best, C. 0.015, 0.02, 0.043, 0.066, 0.026, 0.032, 0.032, 0.042, 0.055, 0.033, 0.032, 0.044, 0.068, and including L, 0.351.

The weld steel, or steely iron, **L** (C. 0.35), when treated by the uniform method usually adopted for chain-cable irons, made the worst welds. Iron **K**, with carbon so low as 0.07, made bad welds, although it was otherwise a good average chain-iron, with a medium amount of impurity. Carbon, in a greater degree than phosphorus, promotes fluidity: hence the iron is "burned" at the ordinary welding temperatures of low-carbon irons.

Slag was highest (2.26 per cent) in the two-inch bar of iron **N**, which welded less soundly than any other bar of the same iron, and below average as compared with the other irons. Slag should theoretically improve welding, like any flux, but its effects in these experiments could not be definitely traced.

WHAT IS LEARNED FROM CHEMICAL ANALYSES.

So far, it may appear that little of use to the makers or the users of wrought-iron has been learned. But it should be remembered that all these irons were intended to be as nearly as possible alike, and to be adapted to the peculiar use of chain-cable. The makers generally understood the necessary conditions, and every effort was made to reach this special standard of excellence. Had it been reached, the irons would have all been exactly alike in physical character, and presumably similar, although not necessarily alike, in chemical character, for certain ingredients may replace others within limits which are perhaps narrow. Certainly the attempt to make all the irons conform to a well-known standard of quality was the worst possible way to ascertain the distinctive effects of the various altering ingredients. In order to make this latter determination, one series of irons should have been made as uniform as possible in all ingredients except one, for instance, phosphorus, and that one should have been varied as much as possible. Another series should have been alike except in silicon; and so on, through the list of altering ingredients. The series of tests which the Board has undertaken on steels was devised upon this principle. It was, however, thought best, after the physical tests of these irons were completed, to subject them to analysis, in the hope that some good result would follow. This hope has been realized in an unexpected and somewhat surprising manner.

1st, The want of uniformity in the chemical composition of the *same brand of iron* is a conspicuous defect which is readily accounted for. In iron **M**, silicon varied from 0.16 to 0.26; in iron **J**, it varied from 0.18 to 0.32. In iron **D**, phosphorus varied from 0.12 to 0.24; and in iron **J**, from 0.14 to 0.29.

Starting with a uniform pig-iron, the puddling process may or may not remove a large amount of silicon, phosphorus, and carbon, according to the temperature and agitation of the bath, the "fix" used in the furnace, and from many causes under the puddler's control, and dependent on his knowledge and skill.

Such variations would be entirely inadmissible in the most common grades of steel: in fact, they could not occur in the cheap steel processes, when using a uniform pig-iron, except by a special effort. In the Bessemer process, the completion of the oxidation of silicon and carbon is obvious to the inexpert observer; in the open-hearth process, unmistakable tests are taken during the operation. The character of steel can be surely predicated on the analysis of its materials; that of wrought-iron is altered by subtle and unobserved causes. Should it be urged in favor of wrought-iron, that P. can be largely removed during its manufacture, while in the steel-manufacture it cannot be, it may be answered that there is an abundance of pig-irons which do not contain much P.; and it is better to be sure of a definite amount of a deleterious ingredient than to run the risk of a variable amount.

We are not prepared to show the exact effect of varying reduction on steel. Ingots of the same grade of steel, from six inches square to fourteen inches square, are employed for the same-sized bars; the larger ones are preferred, notwithstanding the greater cost of working them, not because small ingots will not make good bars: but because they make too much scrap. Steel depends comparatively slightly on condensation for its density, but very greatly on its being cast from a fluid state. It is a crystalline mass in both large and small ingots, and not a bundle of fibres of iron more or less compacted.

2d, This matter of varying strength due to varying reduction — the most important developed by the series of experiments — is made all the more certain and useful by the analyses; for, without a knowledge of the composition of the bars and of the specific effects of different ingredients, a part of the variation now traced to reduction might have been attributed to composition.

It may be stated in general terms, that, notwithstanding this attempt at uniformity, the differences in reduction in the rolling-mill from pile to bar caused as much variation in the physical qualities of these irons as did the differences in the chemical composition of the whole series of irons, excepting the steely iron **L**. The highest difference in tenacity, due apparently to varying reductions, is 11,969 pounds per square inch. The highest difference between the average tensional resistances of all the irons (excepting the steely iron **L**), due to all causes, is but 7,109 pounds. The following illustrations are more in detail: —

Iron P.

	Per Sq. In.
Tenacity of 1 in. bar (1.74 per cent of pile) above 2 in. (6.98 per cent of pile)	6,973 lbs.
Elastic limit " " " " " "	7,352 lbs.

Iron F. Second Lot.

Tenacity of 1¼ in. bar (2.76 per cent of pile) over 2 in. (5.23 per cent of pile)	4,698 lbs.
Elastic limit " " " " " "	3,227 lbs.

Iron F. Third Lot.

Tenacity of ½ in. bar (1.60 per cent of pile) over 2¼ in. (6.13 per cent of pile)	9,656 lbs.
" ⅜ in. bar (3.68 per cent of pile) over 4 in. (15.70 per cent of pile)	7,786 lbs.
Elastic limit of ⅜ in. bar " " " "	15,045 lbs.
Tenacity of 1 in. bar (3.14 per cent of pile) " "	4,806 lbs.

Iron N.

Tenacity of 1¼ in. bar (6.62 per cent of pile) above 2 in. (11.36 per cent of pile) . . 4,395 lbs.

Iron A.

Tenacity of 1 in. bar (3.14 per cent of pile) over 2 in. (8.72 per cent of pile) . . 4,519 lbs.

Iron D.

Difference in phosphorus in 1 in. and 2 in. bars, 0.026; other ingredients about alike.
Tenacity of 1 in. bar over 2 in. bar . . . . 11,969 lbs.

The following are apparently results of composition: —

Comparative Tenacity.

Of iron highest in average qualities over the one lowest in impurities . . . . 3,136 lbs.
Of most tenacious steely iron (carbon 0.35) over least tenacious (carbon 0.04) . . 15,464 lbs.

3d, The variation of welding power by reduction, in a greater degree than by composition, has already been shown in detail. Chemical analyses were necessary to establish this fact.

4th, To the steel maker and user it will appear somewhat remarkable, that phosphorus may run up to nearly a quarter of one per cent in good chain-cable irons, when it is considered that low tenacity and high ductility are the essential features of such irons, and that the effect of this ingredient is to produce exactly opposite results. Suitable working probably counterbalanced its effects.

5th, The comparison of chemical and physical results suggests a number of experiments which would go far to settle vexed questions, and improve the practice, especially with regard to welding.

(1) Regarding slag, it has been shown that a larger amount is sometimes found in a well-worked than in a less-reduced iron, and that its effects are uncertain. Experiments should be arranged to show what composition of slags will readily come out of the pile in rolling; whether two-high or three-high trains will best remove them, and how much and what kind of slag affects strength and welding. A stable oxide of iron, which would probably do the most harm, could be formed by blowing superheated steam upon red-hot bars before piling. It might be proved that very fusible slags, or fluxes, should be placed in the pile to protect surfaces from oxidation, and to wash away less fusible impurities.

(2) It has already been suggested that special irons, having respectively a certain ingredient in excess and the others low and uniform, should be made, in order to ascertain, in a conspicuous manner, the physical effects of the various ingredients.

(3) Referring to a previous recapitulation of remarks on welding: The effects of very different temperatures on irons varying in composition, as compared with that uniformly high temperature usually known as a "welding heat," should be much more carefully ascertained. And the effects, and more especially the means of welding in a non-oxidizing flame, where mobility of surfaces can be got without "burning," should be made the subject of elaborate experiments. The excellent welding of a heterogeneous mass of steel and iron, protected from oxidation by being placed in an iron box which will stand a high heat, has been referred to. The system of gas-welding by which Mr. Bertram welded boilers at Woolwich twenty

years ago has since been in regular use by the Butterly Company, in England, for joining the members of wrought-iron beams of large section. It should seem within the power of modern engineering and chemistry to provide means for the perfection in a non-oxidizing atmosphere, of welds, like those of ships' cables and bridge-links, upon which hang so many lives and so much treasure.

Conclusions Derived from a Comparison of Chemical and Physical Results.

I. Although most of the irons under consideration are much alike in composition, the hardening effects of phosphorus and silicon can be traced, and that of carbon is very obvious. Phosphorus up to 0.10 per cent does not harm, and probably improves, irons containing silicon not above 0.15, and carbon not above 0.03. None of the ingredients except carbon in the proportions present seem to very notably affect welding by ordinary methods.

II. The strength of wrought-iron and its welding power by ordinary methods are varied more by the amount of its reduction in rolling than by its ordinary differences in composition. Uniform strength may be promoted by uniform reduction, but only at such increased cost of manufacture that the practice is not likely to obtain. Therefore the reduced strength of large bars made by ordinary methods should be considered in designing machinery and structures.

III. In accordance with these facts the United-States Test Board has shown, by trial, the unsafety of the Admiralty proof-tables for chain-cable, and has prepared new ones, and also new tables of the strength of different-sized bars. The Board has demonstrated that the tenacity of two-inch bar for chain-cable should be between 48,000 and 52,000 pounds per square inch, and of one-inch bar between 53,000 and 57,000 pounds; and that stronger irons than these make worse cables, because they have low ductility and welding power.

IV. Chemical analyses, made in connection with physical

tests, are indispensable to conclusions about either the character or treatment of iron. In this series of experiments the demonstration that strength is dependent on reduction is made more definite and useful by the analyses.

V. Analyses also prove that the same brand of wrought-iron may be heterogeneous in composition; and they emphasize the previously known fact that wrought-iron making processes, as compared with the cheap steel processes, necessarily give an uncertain character to the former material, while to the latter the desired quality may be imparted with certainty and uniformity.

VI. The ordinary practice of welding is capable of radical improvement: the fact has been fully demonstrated; the means should be made the subject of complete experiments. The perfection of means for welding in a non-oxidizing atmosphere would seem to be the promising direction of improvement.

In submitting the foregoing history of their experiments, and deductions therefrom, the committees recognize the fact that much still remains to be done before either of the investigations can be considered complete. But, having exhausted the time and means at their disposal, they are compelled to submit the results as far as accomplished.

L. A. BEARDSLEE,
Commander U.S.N., Chairman of Committees D, H, and M.

Q. A. GILLMORE,
Lieut.-Col., Corps of Engineers, Brev. Major-Gen., U.S.A., Chairman of Committee B, Member of Committee D.

A. L. HOLLEY, C.E., LL.D.,
Chairman of Committee C, Member of Committee H.

WM. SOOY SMITH, C.E.,
Chairman of Committees E and K, Member of Committees H and M.

DAVID SMITH,
Chief Engineer U.S.N., Chairman of Committee O, Member of Committees D and M.

[NOTE BY THE ABRIDGER.] The committees referred to in the signatures above were charged with the following divisions of the general work of the Board: —

D. On chains and wire rope.
II. On iron, malleable.   } The committees making this report.
M. On re-heating and re-rolling.

B. On armor-plate.
C. On chemical research.   } The reports of these committees
E. On corrosion of metals.   } have not yet been published.
K. On orthogonal simultaneous strains.

www.ingramcontent.com/pod-product-compliance
Lightning Source LLC
Chambersburg PA
CBHW021939160426
43195CB00011B/1156